Spoiled Rotten

Loving Your Kids Without Indulging Them

Ritchie Miller

Spoiled Rotten: Loving Your Kids Without Indulging Them © 2009 Ritchie Miller

ISBN-13978-1-60013-400-5

Printed in the United States of America

10 9 8 7 6 5 4 3 2 1

Acknowledgements

I would like to thank my wife, Kim, for being such a wonderful wife and mother. You are an inspiration to so many, but especially to me. Your encouragement to me over the years has been priceless. I love you dearly.

I would like to thank my three children, Brittney, Brandon, and Brooke, for being great kids. You guys have made my life so much richer. I can't imagine what life would have been without you. You have been the laboratory for all the theories in this book.

I would like to thank my parents, Roger and Linda Miller, for all the wonderful parenting they gave me. Both of you modeled what great parents should look like.

I would like to thank the people of Avalon Church for your pursuit of God and for putting up with me as your pastor. Starting and pastoring this church has been the spiritual highlight of my life.

I would also like to thank my editor, Randall Bonser, for his help in crafting this book. You are a great wordsmith and you turn my scattered ideas into cohesive thoughts.

Table of Contents

Introduction

The Not So Hard Truth

You may want to sit down before you read this. Chances are that you already are sitting down, unless you are one of those crazy people at the gym who try to read while working the Stairmaster. How can you think that you are actually working out if you can read while doing it? But I digress. If you are already sitting down then tighten your belt, get a grip, or do something to prepare yourself for what I am about to reveal. It may be a shocker. Are you ready? Here goes.

It is not easy being a parent today. "But I already know that," you say, "otherwise I would be reading a book about how to get rich selling my unwanted, lame junk to some sucker over the Internet." Actually, I was just testing you; that is not the big surprise. Everybody has been conditioned, at least in our culture, to be nervous about parenting, to think that any little misstep on the parent's part could lead to serious issues in the future. Actually, that kind of psycho-babble, which has kept you on edge for so long, has been great for the publishing industry … but bad for parenting and worse for children.

Here is the real bombshell: *Parenting is not as hard as you think.* The truth is, we often make it harder than it is supposed to be. I believe many parents operate in fear rather than faith, and that is a sure-fire parenting disaster waiting to happen. The good news for all of us is that God, in His instruction manual the Bible, gives us simple, stress-reducing principles that will guide us along this amazing journey.

A Skateboard, a Shock and a Sermon Illustration

One Saturday evening I was walking through my neighborhood. It was almost dark and I walked into one of the cul-de-sacs that are so common in subdivisions in the Atlanta area. What I saw stopped me in my tracks. Something spectacular was about to happen.

Four kids were trying to ride a skateboard from the top of the street down into their driveway about sixty yards away ... *at the same time*. The oldest was a boy about eight years old. He seemed to be in charge of this expedition and was trying to get seated on the back of the skateboard. On the front of the skateboard was a boy, probably six, who was trying to get his feet underneath him so he would not drag his toes. In my mind, he seemed just a little bit too excited about this little trip down injury lane. I could imagine him doing extremely dangerous things one day like bungee-jumping, skydiving or teaching middle school boys. Standing next to them on the curb was a visibly agitated four-year-old boy who had obviously lost the fail proof decision-making game "paper-scissors, rock" and been declared the designated pusher. He had an evil glint in his eye that looked like revenge in the making. Last of all was a two-year-old girl seated in the middle of the skateboard. Her little head was sticking up between the legs of the oldest boy. She looked like a jack-in-the-box and she was squealing with glee and anticipation. The oldest boy had his legs wrapped around the neck of the boy on the front and they were trying to get their balance so they could push off and fly down the hill.

As I assessed the situation, I realized that there was no padding to cushion them, no brake to slow them, no adult to supervise them, and no one to prevent *Revenge Boy* from pushing them as fast as he could down the hill to settle the score of being left off the ride of death. Are you getting the picture? Somebody was about to lose some knuckle and knee skin. There was a high probability of a broken bone, blood, a missing chunk of scalp, loose teeth, and a flood of tears at any second. So, as the only responsible adult around – and a pastor, no less – I did what any responsible man of the cloth would do ... I thought to myself: *This could be a great story for my message on Sunday!* I was not about to stop those kids. Are you kidding me? There were too many good sermon points riding on this potential jaunt to the emergency room.

I held my breath as the impish four-year-old went into action. He gave a colossal shove and the skateboard took off precariously down the hill. He watched them pick up speed for a few seconds, then he took off, too, zigzagging in front of the skateboard to try and knock them over. I was so sure that there was going to be a disaster that I felt like one of those people watching a car crash – you know you should not look but you can't take your eyes off the action. They wobbled and they wiggled and they giggled. They let go of the skateboard and put their hands in the air as they picked up speed, aimed in the general direction of the driveway. As they got close to the bottom of the hill, they were going so fast *Revenge Boy* was having a hard time keeping up with them. They screamed and squealed and yipped like children on the world's greatest roller coaster.

And then it happened. They swooped down at top speed and bumped into the curb and ...stopped. No crash, no blood, no desperate cries for help.

I was so disappointed. These little daredevils had ruined my message so I just turned around and left without another thought. On my way home, however, I had one of those "aha" moments. It occurred to me that this is the *exact picture of parenting that God wants us to see.* Most people see parenting the way they see the rest of the world, seeing danger in every situation. They have coffee, cigarettes, and fingernails for breakfast every morning and they parent just like they live – *constantly expecting a crash.* They base all their decisions on the fear of an undertow rather than an expectation of an overflow. They are gripped by constant dread and no matter how many promises God gives in His instruction manual, they are surprised every day that there is not a crash. And if you think about it, what has all this anxiety accomplished for them? When the inevitable bumps and bruises of life happen, they are still totally unprepared to deal with them.

I don't think God wants us to live that way. We should live with confidence and expectation, believing that God is in control. He wants us to pray and expect His blessings and favor in our lives rather than anticipate a crash. How many times have we spoken something negative into existence just because of the way we look at life? God wants us to live in faith, not fear.

My hope is that this book will be a catalyst to build your faith. I want you to see that you *can* navigate the sometimes turbulent waters of parenting and arrive at your destination without capsizing the boat. I want you to find strength and courage to become the parent God wants you to be. I want you to have confidence in God's instructions.

Oh, and About That 18-Year Money Back Guarantee

Wouldn't it be great if your kids were born with individualized instructions? If you do so many hours of *this* and spend so much time doing *that* and stir it all around for 18 or so years, then – boom! – out comes a fully mature, fully functioning adult! (I've also wished for an 18-year Money Back Guarantee, so that I could return my teenage son to the Manufacturer, but that is another story.) Yes, specific instructions would be a great relief, but we all know our children are as unique as their own set of fingerprints. Fortunately, God has given us an even more effective manual for training our children to be the kind of person *He* wants them to be. Maybe not exactly like we think they ought to be, but definitely the kind of person *He* wants.

So let's get started. Jump on the skateboard and hang on. Better yet, let go and put your hands in the air. It is going to be a fun ride.

CHAPTER ONE
Girls and Boys Gone Wild

Do you remember what it was like before you had kids? I sure do. I had all the answers, even to the questions I had never thought of. If you needed parenting advice, I could help. If you pulled your hair out trying to get your kids to act right in public I had the panacea, the magic potion that would elicit the proper behavior. Problems with your kids? No problem at all. Dr. Miller was in and he was never afraid to prescribe some wisdom.

Then our first child was born. Wow! That sure put a crimp in my pontificating. Before that time, Kim and I had surefire answers for raising kids but no kids. Now we have three kids and no surefire answers.

In fact, before we had children we were pretty sure we had control over our lives. We did fun things, we went to fun places, we cared about the way we looked, we were on time to most things and we even had a house that did not look like a training ground for a career in demolition. But after we had kids, all the easy answers went out the window – and with it, the illusion of control.

If my premise is true, that parenting does not have to be as difficult as everybody makes it seem, then why do we have such a difficult time raising respectful, responsible children? At least, it seems difficult as you're going through it. When they are toddlers, your vocabulary goes from a few thousand words to a few dozen and 76.3 percent of your sentences include the words "no" or "don't."

When they are in elementary school you are tempted to yank out your follicles in large chunks as they whine, fight with their siblings and say, "I don't know" to every question you ask. You feel like your head will explode if you have to tell them one more time to pick up their toys, eat their vegetables, stop calling their sister names, do their homework, turn off the video game or keep their feet off of the ceiling. You ask insane questions because they make you crazy. "Do you want a spanking?" Who in their right mind wants a spanking? But we ask and then if they are brave or crazy enough to answer we get even more perturbed.

Then they become teenagers and you worry about music, friends, college, piercings, tattoos, attitudes and becoming a grandparent too early. You fluctuate between worrying that they might actually run away from home and fantasizing about the day they finally move out. At this stage, you go back to saying "No" in about half your sentences.

"So what gives?" you ask. "How could it possibly be easier than I think when having a peaceful day is a minor miracle?"

The Disease

The reason that parenting seems so difficult lies in one simple but significant fact – your child was born with a sin nature. This historical and spiritual truth comes to us from the Bible, which tells us that we all sin and constantly fall short of God's divine standards.[1] Sin is a disease that poisons everything on earth, including relationships.

But God's instruction manual also teaches that there is a fairly simple cure to the problems of parenting. Instead of some complicated set of rules to follow, the Bible says that our primary job is to point our children toward the correct destination – or target, which is a word picture I'll talk about in the next chapter – and that destination is Jesus Christ. That is your main job, plain and simple.

Contrary to what your neighbors and the media are telling you, that simple job is more important than education, manners, athletics, little league and

---

[1] Romans 3:23

good nutrition. I learned a long time ago that discovering what God expects from you will ease your stress levels and give you hope. Over the next several chapters, we will talk about how you can guide your children to their most important destination. But before we do that, I would like to explain a little further where parenting problems come from in the first place.

The First Generational Conflict

God tells us that it takes faith and wisdom to train your children. Solomon wrote, "A house is built by wisdom and becomes strong through good sense" (Proverbs 24:3, NLT). I think it is critical to understand that your difficulty in raising godly kids did not begin with your generation. It did not begin because of some mistake you made in the past. The reality is, parenting problems began in the Garden of Eden.

Before Adam and Eve sinned, there was no sin and no curse. Everything was perfect. Think about how different being a parent would be if you did not have to deal with arguing, fighting, selfishness and disobedience. But when Adam and Eve sinned, God placed a curse on everything. He cursed the serpent, mankind, and even the earth.

> Then the LORD God said to the serpent, "Because you have done this, you are cursed more than all animals, domestic and wild. You will crawl on your belly, groveling in the dust as long as you live. And I will cause hostility between you and the woman, and between your offspring and her offspring. He will strike your head, and you will strike his heel."
>
> Then he said to the woman, "I will sharpen the pain of your pregnancy, and in pain you will give birth. And you will desire to control your husband, but he will rule over you."
>
> And to the man he said, "Since you listened to your wife and ate from the tree whose fruit I commanded you not to eat, the ground is cursed because of you. All your life you will struggle to scratch a living from it. It will grow thorns and thistles for you, though you will eat of its grains. By the sweat of your brow will

you have food to eat until you return to the ground from which you were made. For you were made from dust, and to dust you will return" (Genesis 3:14-19).

As a consequence of this sin, we experience four powerful struggles:

- ***The struggle with sin.*** Sin has infected all of us. We are born with a sin nature and as a result we experience – and cause – conflict. Many of our personal, internal conflicts are a result of the struggle with sin.
- ***The struggle with children.*** As a part of the curse, God told Eve that she would struggle in childbirth. The pain in bearing children doesn't end when the child is born; it continues throughout our lives. Struggles with our children began with sin in the Garden of Eden.
- ***The struggle with marriage.*** God also told Eve that part of the curse would be that she would desire to control her husband, but that he would rule over her.[2] That pronouncement foreshadowed the first problems in a marriage – see, you're not alone! Marriage has been a struggle ever since. You can't have a perfect marriage but you can have the peace that comes with a marriage that is blessed by God.
- ***The struggle with work.*** God also told Adam that the ground would be cursed because of his sin. Because it would produce thorns and weeds, he would now have to scratch out a living by the sweat of his brow. Thus began our struggle with work.

The Cure

A bestselling book popular right now preaches the message that religion poisons everything. The truth is that the disease of sin poisons everything. We commonly think of disobedience to God as being the very first sin, but why did Adam and Eve disobey? Wasn't it because they didn't trust God's plan? They had a better idea, so they formulated their own plan. Not trusting God's plan for our lives and parenting is still at the root of all of our parenting disasters.

---

[2] Genesis 3:16

But this passage in Genesis also gives us the clue to overcoming each of these struggles. It says that God made a sacrifice. He sacrificed an animal to make coats of skin, which represented the fact that Jesus would one day be the sacrifice for all sin. In this, we find the answer to all of our struggles. *It is a relationship with God.* This alone has the single greatest impact on what kind of parent you will be.

CHAPTER TWO

Good Parenting Begins with Papa

I can remember the powerful feelings I had when each of our three children was born. Brittney is our eldest and when she was born, I was the first to hold her and I had never experienced the depth of emotion I felt at that moment. I knew that I was going to love this person for the rest of my life. I promised her right then and there that I would do anything in my power to protect her. She truly was the most beautiful baby I had ever seen.

Nine months later, we found out we were expecting again. After the ultrasound, when we found out that we were having a baby boy, I was so proud. Every dad wants a son and I could not wait. When the time came time for him to be born, I was overwhelmed with anticipation. When Brandon was born, though, I thought he looked like a lizard. I really thought something was wrong with him. I am not making that up. I honestly thought that there had been a mix up in the delivery room and that they had accidentally switched our beautiful baby with some ugly peoples' baby. When the shock of what he looked like wore off, I came to my senses and promised Brandon that I would try to be the best father I could possibly be to him. I promised to teach him how to be a man. I knew that I was going to be so proud of him. Thankfully, he looked a lot better after a few months.

When Brooke, our youngest daughter, was born, she, like her sister, was the most beautiful baby I had ever seen. She was God's surprise to us. I remember feeling so happy that God had given her to us. As I held her, I imagined her as a toddler, then as a child and finally as a teenager. That's when I began to get grouchy, thinking about how all the boys who will like her in the future will try to speak to her and come calling at our house to try and take her out. I immediately told her that she could not date until she was 31 ½ years old. After I calmed down, I promised her that I would never let any harm come to her and that I would protect her all my life.

The Truth Starts to Hurt

But somewhere along the way reality set in. Those fantasies about perfect children and perfect parenting flew out the window with the first temper tantrum. I quickly realized that my greatest joy in life was also going to be my greatest challenge.

I wish I knew then what I know now. Not a formula or an activity that would guarantee perfect children — but a promise that guarantees perfect peace. We have to keep in mind that even though having children is a challenge, you can be a good parent — in fact, you are just the parent God had in mind. God chose to give your kids *to* you so that they would turn out right. Knowing that, I think you can understand why I say that your job is quite possibly less complex than you think.

In the last chapter, we learned that *our children have a sin nature*. The next big truth we must realize in order to raise godly, respectful, well-adjusted kids is just as simple but just as profound: **good parenting grows from a good relationship with God**. It all begins with Papa, Abba -- our Heavenly Father. I love what the Psalmist said:

> Unless the Lord builds a house, the work of the builders is useless. Unless the Lord protects a city, guarding it with sentries will do no good. It is useless for you to work so hard from early morning until late at night, anxiously working for food to eat; for God gives rest to his loved ones. Children are a gift from the Lord; they are a reward from him. Children born to a young man are like sharp arrows in a warrior's hands. How happy is the man whose

quiver is full of them! He will not be put to shame when he confronts his accusers at the city gates (Psalm 127:1-5).

I want to point out a couple of very important truths from these verses. God gives us two powerful metaphors in this psalm. First, building a family is like building a house. If we try to build a godly household apart from the truth of God's word, we are wasting our time.

Second, we see a word picture of children as arrows in a warrior's hands. Parents are the warriors and children are the arrows. The primary job of the warrior is to make sure that the arrow hits the target; otherwise, his arrows are useless. Do you get the picture? Your primary job as a parent is to get your children to the right destination, or target. What is the target? A degree in medicine? A large house in the suburbs? While those things may be desirable, the destination here is a relationship with God, or to be more specific, a relationship with Jesus Christ. Education, wealth, health and manners are important but they are not the most important. The most important thing you can do for your child is to point her to the correct target.

Thinking of parenting in this way certainly makes our job much simpler. If we are going to be effective warriors, however, we need to pay attention to some important "shooting lessons."

Everything I Need to Know About Parenting I Learned at Summer Camp

The first shooting lesson seems obvious: an arrow must be taken out of the quiver to fulfill its purpose. While it's true that arrows that stay in the quiver will never embarrass us or fail miserably, those quiver-dwellers will also never fulfill their purpose in life. Our job as parents is to prepare our children to leave our home eventually and to start their own.

An arrow can't be controlled, it must be released. Wouldn't it be strange to see a warrior running alongside the arrow, making sure its path was straight? Or worse yet, carrying the arrow to the target and trying to jam it in? That would be dumb and possibly fatal. No, an arrow is supposed to be released. That is what it is made for. To paraphrase a saying from the world of hockey, no arrow that is not released will effectively hit its target. Will every arrow always hit perfectly in the center of the bull's-eye? Of course not. That's why you must trust God with the outcome.

The second shooting lesson is just as obvious, but just as important: an arrow must be aimed properly in order to hit the target. If you take aim at the wrong thing, you can do more harm than good. In a battle, warriors don't aim at random targets, but at specifically chosen ones. A warrior can be successful in nailing his target right in the sweet spot, but if has selected the wrong target, his work is all in vain. In the same way, we can act "target challenged" when we get our children involved in every activity under the sun except those that teach them to honor God.

Lesson three: an arrow must be released at the right time in order to hit the target. Even if your bow is in line with the right target, the arrow will never hit the bull's-eye if you release it at the wrong time. I know this from lessons I learned the hard way at summer camp ... right in front of the girls I was trying to impress. Release it too early and it will be lodged in the ground; release it too late and it will sail over the target. We must release our children to God, but we must also let go at the right time.

But the Sun Was In My Eyes

You'll know you've hit the target in that magical moment when your child commits his life completely to the Lord. To achieve that, you've got to take out the arrow, point it at the right target and let it go at the proper time. If you have older children, you've probably already figured out that you cannot control your child's relationship with God. But you can create the right conditions for a clean shot by making sure your own relationship with God is healthy and growing.

God has already initiated a relationship with us. That relationship will grow when we get to know Him and when we obey him. We get to know Him through reading and learning about the Bible, praying, worshipping Him in corporate worship with other believers, serving Him by serving others through a local church, giving of our time and financial resources, and doing life with Christian friends in small groups.

I like what I heard one pastor say, when asked why his sermons weren't "meatier." He said: "the meat is in the street." In other words, we grow deep in our relationship with God by actively engaging in the Christian life, not by passively sitting and soaking up facts about the Bible. This kind of growing relationship with God provides the answers for every struggle we face – sin, children, marriage and work. When we obey God and follow His plan for us, it becomes clear what we are to do in every area of our lives, including dealing with our children.

I am not suggesting that just because you go to church that your children will automatically love God. We know that is not true by simple observation. I am saying that establishing a growing and active relationship with God, where Christ is at the center of all that you do, is the most important job you have as a parent. You can't force your child to know and love God, but you sure can lead them with your passion and transparency. Good parenting grows from a good relationship with God.

"Wait a minute," you say, "are you saying that only religious people can be good parents?" No, I am not saying that. There certainly are people who had a poor or nonexistent relationship with God who have done an adequate job – even an admirable job – of raising their children. Nor I am not suggesting that every parent who has a relationship with God gets it right all the time. I am saying that the *only* way to parent *God's way* is through a relationship with our Creator. That relationship is the foundation for overcoming all the struggles we face –with sin, children, marriage and work.

When we fail to get to know God and His instructions from the Bible on dealing with our children, we do exactly what Adam and Eve did in the Garden of Eden – we formulate our own plan. What happens when we formulate our own plan rather than follow God's? We drop the cheese out of our sandwich. We struggle. We sin. We come up with ideas for parenting that do more harm than good. We follow popular culture and even begin to doubt the parenting advice we find in Scripture.

Aiming at the right target is critical for your children to turn out the way God wants. Solomon in his wisdom told us to *"point your kids in the right direction—when they're old they won't be lost"* (Proverbs 22:6 The Message). Aim your children at the right target. Point them to the correct destination. It makes the job of being a parent a lot less complex, doesn't it?

CHAPTER THREE
God's Parenting Pyramid

One of the things that I love about the Bible is that it is filled with stories of real people who had flaws, warts and struggles just like you and me. Many Christians, who've never read the Bible carefully, believe that these stories are about superheroes that all live happily ever after. Just like us, people in the Bible struggled with following God perfectly. That's why it is important to remember that, while I am giving you some perfect truths and principles from the Bible, there are no perfect parents or perfect children.

I have never tried to hide the fact that my wife and I are imperfect people and imperfect parents. We have imperfect children. We never try to suggest that we get it right all the time. But the good news is that, while we won't achieve perfection until we get to heaven, we can have a blessed and happy family here on earth. Not flawless, but protected by God. Not a fairy tale, but successful, confident and complete. We can find the hope that comes from God's help.

God has some wonderful things to say about how you can have that kind of family. In Deuteronomy chapter six, Moses gives a speech to the nation of Israel. He is closing in on his last days of leading God's people and he is repeating what he considers to be the most important things they need to remember. In a nutshell, he tells them to prioritize their relationship with God and to teach their children how to have a relationship with God. Here is part of what he says:

> "Listen, O Israel! The LORD is our God, the LORD alone. And you must love the LORD your God with all your heart, all your soul, and all your strength. And you must commit yourselves wholeheartedly to these commands that I am giving you today. Repeat them again and again to your children. Talk about them when you are at home and when you are on the road, when you are going to bed and when you are getting up. Tie them to your hands and wear them on your forehead as reminders. Write them on the doorposts of your house and on your gates. (Deuteronomy 6:4-9).

I want to show you, from this passage, what I believe to be some foundational principles for being a good parent. There are many principles in this speech, but I want to focus on three practical applications for parenting young children and teens.

The Power of the Pyramid

Imagine building a pyramid. In order for it to be functional it must be built from the foundation up. You can't start in the middle, then work north and south. And you can't start at the top and continue downward. For a pyramid to stand, it must be built in a certain order and in a certain way. Parenting is much the same. You have to begin with a solid foundation and build up from there.

The foundation of the pyramid is **respect for authority**. Moses said, "Listen, O Israel! The LORD is our God, the LORD alone." There is an absolute and concrete quality to that statement, isn't there? This strong statement of who God is and how He relates to me greatly affects my parenting.

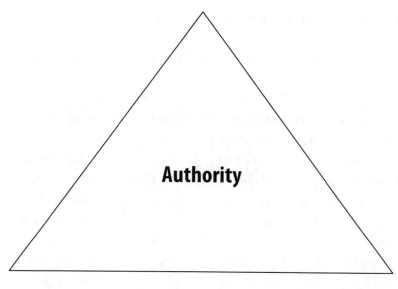

Illustration: 1

In a later chapter we will further develop the idea of how parental authority relates to effective discipline. For now I want you to focus on how important it is for you to develop a proper relationship with God in order to be a good parent. Moses, the writer of Deuteronomy, makes this clear in the passage we just read. He doesn't beat around the bush – he says that you must obey God and have a relationship with Him in order to be blessed in your family. Why is this important? Because it gives you the authority to lead!

Without the foundation of truth and righteousness, which only come from a perfectly just God, you will never be able to point your children to the *"why."* Why should I listen to you? Why should I do what you say? Why should I follow your directions? With this in mind, the old shirt that parents of toddlers used to wear that says, "Because I said so" is no meaningless cliché – it's based on spiritual truth. Lacking this concrete foundation, when your children become adults they will be more likely to wallow in relativism, fail to set boundaries in their relationships, and have trouble discovering their purpose in life. There is a great sense of security that comes from knowing the all-powerful God loves us enough to give us concrete, authoritative principles by which to live. This knowledge transformed the Israelites and it will transform you when you truly grasp it.

Here's how one writer describes how this knowledge helped shape a whole nation:

> *This verse has been called the Shema, from the Hebrew word translated* **Hear.** *The statement in this verse is the basic confession of faith in Judaism. The verse means that the* **LORD** *(Yahweh) is totally unique. He alone is* **God.** *The Israelites could therefore have a sense of security that was totally impossible for their polytheistic neighbors. The "gods" of the ancient Near East rarely were thought of as acting in harmony. Each god was unpredictable and morally capricious. So a pagan worshiper could never be sure that his loyalty to one god would serve to protect him from the capricious wrath of another. The monotheistic doctrine of the Israelites lifted them out of this insecurity since they had to deal with only one God, who dealt with them by a revealed consistent righteous standard.* [3]

While I love our country, I believe that concept of "rugged individualism" that we so admire may hinder many of us from establishing a proper relationship to God, our ultimate Authority. That may be why so many of us struggle with establishing a proper authority hierarchy with our own children. We want to be respected in our homes but we don't show the same submission to God. It is tempting to build our parenting foundation on something other than respect for authority. We try to build it on the idea of friendship with our kids, or the development of abstract reasoning, or on the fool's gold of gift-giving. These foundations are all destined to crumble when life becomes stormy.

When a child is young, you can be all those things – a friend, a philosopher and a Santa Clause, but the guiding principle of your parenting must be on

---

[3] Walvoord, J. F., Zuck, R. B, *The Bible Knowledge Commentary : An Exposition of the Scriptures* (Wheaton, IL: Victor Books, 2004), p.274.

teaching concrete absolutes. Trying to develop complex concepts is futile with toddlers and young children. How many times have you witnessed a parent in a public place trying her best to get through to her little one by explaining "why it is bad to break the pickle jars," only to be met by screaming and crying and stomping feet (and broken pickle jars)? When children are small they have to learn to do what you tell them because *you are the authority in their life.*

A Solid Midsection

Next on the parenting pyramid is understanding abstract concepts through *teaching.*

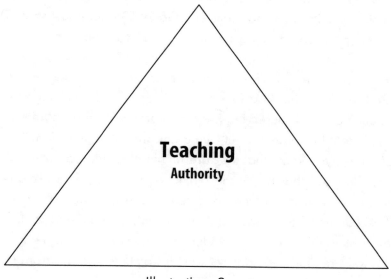

Teaching
Authority

Illustration: 2

Once you have established parental authority in their early years, then you spend more time teaching abstract concepts, or reasoning, as they get older. During the preteen and teenage years is when this is most effective. Notice that God said to repeat these things again and again and to talk about them in your everyday life. I believe you have to live it, love it and sometimes laugh at it. Kim and I began to understand this concept better when our son, Brandon, was in middle school. Please forgive me for telling so many stories about

Brandon. We really do love him and I am not picking on him but, of our three children, he gave us the most opportunities to work on our parenting skills. (Plus, Brittney and Brooke would not give me permission to share as many stories)

We repeatedly told Brandon that he must do things just because we said to do them. By this point he totally got the idea of parental authority. We needed to teach him more about the concept of consequences, though. Occasionally, he would forget what we told him to do and one of us would bail him out. It was definitely time for us to move from the *concrete* idea authority to the *concept* of learning the consequences of your behavior.

While driving one day I got a frantic call from Kim. She was about forty-five minutes away from our house and Brittney, who was thirteen at the time, called her and simply said in her normally calm tone, "Brandon just shot himself and he is bleeding." I probably do not have to tell you that Kim and I were very concerned.

I arrived at our house in a matter of just a couple of minutes and discovered that Brandon had found a package of nail gun blanks behind our church building. He brought the package home with him and decided that he would explode it by hammering it with a hammer. If you are familiar with these kinds of blanks you know that they are nothing less than a bullet with the lead removed. I learned that he hit the blanks and one of them exploded into his wrist barely missing his arteries and tendons. There was blood everywhere. When I asked him what he was thinking he looked at me and said, "But I put a piece of newspaper over it." I wonder how many more stitches it would have taken if it were not for the sports section? It was time to move from the *concrete* to the *concept* with Brandon.

Many parents discover too late that they have reversed the order in the parenting pyramid. When their children are toddlers they try and explain their way out of problems, and when the kids become teenagers and ask "why?" they tend to lose their cool and yell, "Because I said so!" Often, relationship struggles between parents and teens stem from building on the wrong foundation. As kids get older we must move from our position of authority into a position of authoritative teaching.

Not So Lonely at the Top

As our not-so-little ones become adults (put the tissue down, there's no crying in baseball or parenting books), we should move to the final and crowning part of the parenting pyramid - *confidence*.

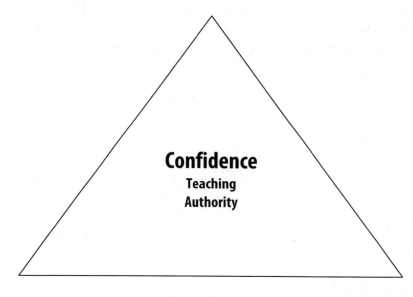

Confidence
Teaching
Authority

Illustration: 3

This is the point – and the reward – of godly parenting. The goal is to help our children become well-adjusted, responsible, godly adults who operate out of their own set of core beliefs and convictions. Granted, you can't make your children love Jesus. There are going to be times that they disappoint you. There will be times that they fail to hit that bull's-eye toward which you'ves done your best to aim them. Remember, there are no perfect children, and certainly no perfect parents. But while you can't make them love God, I do believe you can create an environment that causes them to *not* love God. You can go to church and still create an environment that leads to doubt. When we ignore the clear teachings of the Bible, fail to serve, refuse to participate in life-changing small groups, and complain about the emphasis on money and giving we are robbing our children of the example they deserve.

If you follow God's plan you can have confidence. Your confidence must come from your relationship to your Heavenly Father – which, incidentally, is built on the same pyramid structure as the one you're trying to build with your children – not from how successful your children look at the age of 21. Remember, God was the only perfect parent and Adam and Eve still sinned. So our confidence must come from the fact that we are obeying Him to the best of our ability. When you let God call the shots in your life, then you gain the right – and the confidence – to call the rights shots in your children's lives.

Chapter FOUR
Who Calls the Shots?
Power Struggles at Home

I grew up in Mt. Airy, North Carolina. That is where the beloved television character Andy Griffith lived, the setting for the fictional town of Mayberry. Mayberry was the sleepy little town where no one was ever in a hurry and Andy always found a way for everyone to get along. Things were perfect in Mayberry. Kids always obeyed their parents. The good citizens were always safe and no one ever had a bad day. Contrast that with the real world and you quickly realize that Mayberry is purely fictional. After all, Mt. Airy is the place where, as a twelve-year-old, I drove my grandfather's truck half way through a muddy field until it sank up to the axles in mud. The violence and language aimed at me after that stunt would never make it past the censors on the Andy Griffith Show.

In the real world, good and bad people alike fight stress from work, financial pressures, worries about children, divorce, blended families, single parent households, loneliness, little league snack schedules and the list could go on. Even Christians don't get a free pass. Once I saw a guy with a bumper sticker that read "Honk If You Love Jesus." I blew my horn at the guy as I passed him on the Interstate and he promptly gave me the old one-digit-wave, flipped me the tall-man-salute, shot me a bird, or whatever you call it in your section of the country. We all hope our families will be a refuge from the stress of the world, but in many cases they become our biggest source of stress. Managing your family life, whether you are married, have a blended family, a single parent family or are divorced is a real challenge.

You may still think I'm crazy for saying this, but hopefully it's becoming clearer why I made the declaration that good parenting does not have to be as hard as we think. One of the best ways to make parenting easier is to make sure that you, the parent, call the shots in the home. I think this is a serious problem in many homes today. Parents have abdicated their role and responsibility to their children. In the average home the kid is calling the shots! No wonder so many parents struggle and think parenting is a nightmare. You think the U.S. financial industry is in a state of chaos? Just let your kids run your life – you'll wish for your own sanity bailout!

Children need the covering of parental authority to learn about the world in the freedom of an environment where their mistakes are not going to cause them – and us – permanent damage. God never intended for children to be in charge of the home. His plan is for parents to lead from a place of God-given authority. The Apostle Paul wrote, *"Parents, do not treat your children in such a way as to make them angry. Instead, bring them up with Christian discipline and instruction"* (Ephesians 6:4 Good News Translation). This shows us that **you** are to be in charge in the home, not your children. Once again, Solomon wrote, *"Children just naturally do silly, careless things, but a good spanking will teach them how to behave"* (Proverbs 22:15, GNT).

Parenting Styles that Lead to Power Struggles

What happens when we formulate our own plan rather than follow God's? We struggle to maintain a parenting structure that leads to success for our children. We adopt parenting styles that do not work, with the result that we end up turning the reins of authority in the home over to our kids. Here are a few of these styles; hopefully you will find both humor and truth in them. As I heard one pastor say, "If you can't say "Amen," you can say "Ouch!"

The Rescuer

This is the parent that goes beyond the normal parameters of protecting and guiding their children. She becomes a rescuer – I call her The 911 Parent - who rushes in and rescues her child from every scrape, every conflict, every trouble and every problem. This parent can be seen yelling at teachers, coaches, youth pastors, other parents, and eventually at attorneys, judges and parole officers. Her children tend to think that everyone owes them something and have a problem accepting responsibility for their actions. And why shouldn't they? Mommy has always shielded them from the consequences of their actions.

The Chauffeur

This parent tries to live vicariously through his son or daughter. He is sometimes called the American Idol Parent or the All-American Parent. He is convinced that being a good parent means that every second of a child's day must be filled with activity. Through cheerleading, dance, karate, music, softball and every other activity imaginable, his goal is to make his child a superstar. The Chauffeur's obsession goes beyond the child's interest or family fun. He runs a child-centered household and can be seen eight nights a week at ballparks, gyms, studios, fast-food restaurants, gas-pumps and ATMs, as he spends more money trying to earn a scholarship for his child than it would take to pay for ten years of college.

The Buddy

This parent is a big fan of the CB Radio, as his motto is "10-4, good buddy." He is convinced that he must be buddy-buddy with his kids at all costs. His quest to be the coolest dad prevents him from ever really taking control of his home. Strangely, this parenting style often does not lead to closer relationships but to deep hurt and resentment. These parents can often be found sitting by the phone waiting for a call from their kids or in their therapist's office.

The Negotiator

The negotiator tries to reason with an unreasonable toddler. She is convinced that preschool children can rationally come to their own conclusions about interpersonal relationship dynamics. The negotiator has been known to bribe with promises of ice cream, money, toys and eventually new cars for a sixteenth birthday. She can often be found chasing children through the mall or cleaning up broken pickle jars in the grocery store.

The Philanthropist

This parent is often mistaken for Santa Claus because of all the gifts he gives. Because he feels overwhelming guilt for his past mistakes or his frequent absence from the home, he morphs into the jolly old guy with the belief that he can buy some love. Single parents and those from blended families often believe that through permissiveness and gift giving they can recreate the joy of Christmas every weekend. These parents are often on a first name basis with the cashier at Toys-R-Us.

The Super Hero

This parent is under the assumption that she can do it all. She has super powers that enable her to focus unlimited amounts of time on her career, her looks, her hobbies, her children's classroom, and her husband. She can usually be found passed out on top of the covers with her shoes on.

Orchestrate a Hostile Takeover

There are no perfect parents but you can be a parent that operates according to God's rules. Whether you are a parent of a newborn and have not had a chance to screw up yet, or if you are living with the strife that comes from allowing your children to rule the roost for a while, there is hope! You can take back the reins of your household and have a blessed family. Starting out right is easier, of course, but if you have allowed your authority to slip, here is how you can get it back.

My Daddy is Bigger Than Your Daddy

Your authority comes from God. Remember that! Whenever you doubt, go back to Deuteronomy chapter six and remind yourself that your authority comes from your relationship with God. It is important that you invoke what God says with your children. Remind them that you have been given authority by God and that you take your responsibility seriously.

Not only do you have a serious responsibility to lead from authority as a parent, your children have a serious responsibility to follow your leadership. Ephesians 6:1 says, *"Children, obey your parents because you belong to the Lord, for this is the right thing to do."*

Follow God's Divine Order

If you are going to have a God-centered and parent-led home, you must follow God's plan for the home. It is easy to get our priorities out of order. So many voices compete with what the Bible teaches about the home that it is sometimes hard *not* to get distracted. God's order is very simple. He teaches us to prioritize this way:

- Our relationship with God comes first,
- Our marriage is our second priority, then
- Our children are third on the list.

If you are going to lead your home rather than allowing your children or the false idols of popular culture to lead your home, you **must** follow this pattern of priorities.

Our relationship with God is what gives us our authority to lead, but our relationship with our spouse gives us a foundation of loyalty, trust and affection that speaks volumes to our children. I know many parents – especially moms – who disagree with this order. Their children come first and everyone – especially their husbands – know it.

Making the marriage a priority helps you maintain a united front when it comes to leading the home and enforcing discipline. A healthy marriage also gives your children comfort and creates a stable environment by modeling unconditional love. The Bible is very clear that we are to love and serve our spouse and to love, teach, discipline *and release* our children. In the child-centered home, the parents often drift apart and cease to love and serve each other like they should. Intimacy suffers and ultimately so do the children.

Putting children third on our list of priorities does not mean that we love them any less. It simply means that we are following God's plan and are helping prepare them to be responsible and respectful adults who please God with the way they live.

Be Large and in Charge

If you have abdicated the throne in your home, you will have to make a conscious effort to regain it. Becoming a leader is not easy at first, but it pays great dividends later. The choice is yours – you can lead now and reap the benefits of a child who respects authority, or take the easy route and suffer the long-term damage to the relationship between you and your child. The Bible teaches that abdicating parental leadership will greatly hinder your child's ability to become a productive member of society. You and your child will always win when you decide to lead your home God's way.

Prepare for Combat

Not every child gives up the reins easily. You probably know from experience that children are self-centered and determined to have their own way. And some are more determined than others to make the rules in the household. You have to be even more determined than they are to stay the course of biblical leadership.

You Think You Have a Willful Child?

When our son, Brandon, was a toddler he was the most strong-willed person I have ever encountered. We had almost daily battles over who was going to be in charge. Kim and I had to be strong or he would have made our house very "Brandon-centered." For those of you who are battling a little monster like that now, I want to encourage you: there is hope if you stay the course! I am not saying that we never doubted, because there was a time that I thought either Brandon or I would end up in jail and I was not sure which one of us it would be.

One of those times was when Brandon was just shy of three years old. He was sitting in his chair eating lunch when Kim gave him a new little toy to play with. We had a strict rule that if you did not say "thank you," whatever you had been given would be taken away until you showed proper appreciation. On this particular day, the punishment went beyond the norm because he became willfully defiant and challenged my authority. I punished him appropriately and sat him back in his chair and told him that he still had to say "thank you" before he left the table. That's when it turned into World War III. He adamantly refused and the punishment was obviously having no effect on him. We decided to take it to another level.

About that time Kim came through the kitchen and announced that she was taking Brittney, our oldest daughter, to her mother's house. Brandon began to cry and say that he wanted to go to "Nanny's" house. So I picked him up, walked over to the couch, sat him on my lap and told him that as soon as he said "thank you" that I would take him to his grandmother's house.

A colossal power struggle ensued for the leadership of our household. He began to wiggle and cry and yell, *"I don't want to say thank you, I want to go to Nanny's house."* I calmly told him that he could go just as soon as he said "thank you."

For one solid hour he cried, tried to get down and yelled, *"I don't want to say thank you, I want to go to Nanny's house."* Every time he said it I repeated that he could go as soon as he obeyed the rules. During that hour he almost lost his voice and I almost lost my mind. Finally, he stopped wiggling and crying, took a deep breath, and looked at me with an amused look his face and said, "Thank you. Can I go to Nanny's house now?" Of course, I said yes. I wanted someone else to deal with him for a while!

Please notice that leadership doesn't mean violence or abuse. While I believe that there is a place for moderate corporal punishment, becoming the leader in your home is never an excuse to intimidate or abuse your children, either physically or emotionally.

When You Get in Over Your Head Reach Up

Like every other parent, you will sometimes feel like you are in over your head. That is completely normal. When you get in over your head, you need to reach up, because your Heavenly Father is waiting to help you.

I am not much of a fisherman, because unless the fish are jumping into the boat, I get bored quickly. The first time I ever recall going fishing was when I was about six years old. My dad tried to teach me how to bait a hook. The bait is what lures or tempts the fish. This is how it works: the big fish is just minding his own business, swimming along, checking out the girl fish, flexing his fins, when suddenly he sees a tempting worm just floating by. He doesn't realize that if he takes the bait he is going to be a meal himself.

I tried fishing for a little while, but being six years old, I didn't have too much patience for drowning worms. But I did find a little frog to be quite interesting. In fact, I liked him so much that I tried to catch him. I squatted down and reached out for the little fellow. That frog became "bait" for me. I was being lured away from my father's side.

The frog hopped and I hopped. The frog hopped a little farther and I hopped a little farther. You get the picture. We were having a grand time, but there was one little problem – frogs are amphibians. They are quite at home in the water. Six-year-old boys who can't swim are not amphibian. So there I was, being tempted by this little frog that was headed toward a dangerous place – a deep lake. But I did not think about the consequences of following my little friend. I just wanted to catch him and have more fun than I was having learning the finer points of being a fisherman. Before I knew it, this frog had hopped right into the water and without thinking I hopped right in after him. This did not bother him at all because he was supposed to be in the water, but when I hopped in I began to sink right away. The water was way over my head and I quickly lost sight of my father.

That was an odd feeling. I felt like I was in slow motion. I could not hear or see anything. When I realized that I could not breathe I got really scared and instinctually reached up. I could not see but I was reaching up nonetheless. Fortunately my dad saw what happened and came running over to where I had fallen in. He reached right in – without trying to teach me a lesson first – and pulled me to safety. I was really glad to have a dad that rescued me when I was scared and took me into his arms even when I messed up by following my "temptation."

Whenever you feel tempted to give up, don't. If you get scared because you are not sure if you are doing the right thing as a parent, then just reach up. You have a Heavenly Father that sees you and He is reaching down to rescue you and take you in His arms.

CHAPTER FIVE
Lord, Give Me Patience:
Communicating with Love

Communicating to your children with love is a lifelong learning process. Some parents seem to have an easier time with this than others but we all have to learn to be effective communicators. You may find that communicating with your children is easier in some stages of growth than others. Kim found it much easier to communicate with our children during their preschool and preteen years. She does not care for the sarcastic and unpredictable way that teenagers converse or for their undulating and dramatic episodes.

I, on the other hand, have found it easier to communicate during the teenage years. Kim says that is because I still act like an adolescent. The first time she told me that, I threw down my Bible commentary and yelled, "That's, like, so totally unfair!" and stormed out, slammed my bedroom door and pouted.

Maybe I find it harder to communicate with younger children because I have trouble answering their questions. When our oldest daughter, Brittney, was in first grade she asked me one of the hardest questions I've ever encountered. She looked up at me with her big, blue, innocent eyes and asked, "Daddy, why did God make mommies with two breasts and not just one?" I did not know what to say. I had never really thought about it. All I knew was that I was really glad that God did decide to create women that way. Almost everything I could think of seemed inappropriate to say to my innocent little girl. That's when our son, Brandon, who was four at the time, bailed me out. He said in his most disgusted-with-how-dumb-you-are voice, "Everybody knows that, Brittney!" I was praying that he did not look at me because he would have come to the realization that I did not have a clue. He still thought that dads were the most awesome, all-knowing, all-powerful creatures in the world and I did not want to shatter his illusion.

I could hardly wait to hear the acumen of my four-year-old son concerning female anatomy. He said, "Everybody knows that's how mommies feed their babies." He looked at me with a knowing nod like he was getting ready to give the answer to the meaning of life and continued, "So God gave mommies two breasts so while one is emptying out the other one is filling up." I still don't know if that is the right answer or not but it is still better than any explanation that I can give. Little kids ask questions that are way out of my league. I am better at answering teenage questions because they are so much simpler to answer. *"Can I borrow the car?" "Can I have some money?" "Can I stay out late tonight?"* Saying "No" is much easier than trying to explain why mommies have two breasts.

Many passages in the New Testament talk about communicating, but one in particular is helpful in guiding our communication with our children.

> *Love is patient and kind. Love is not jealous or boastful or proud or rude. It does not demand its own way. It is not irritable, and it keeps no record of being wronged. It does not rejoice about injustice but rejoices whenever the truth wins out. Love never gives up, never loses faith, is always hopeful, and endures through every circumstance (I Corinthians 13:4-7).*

This Might Take A While

The Apostle Paul, the writer of First Corinthians, tells us that *love is patient.* Learning to communicate with your children in a loving and Christ like manner will take time. Don't get frustrated. Every parent has a difficult time at some point feeling like they are making a real connection with their kids. Be patient.

Remember, things may seem difficult but it does not have to be as hard or laborious as the secular publishing industry wants you to believe.

An important aspect of the kind of love we are talking about is *time*. Spending time together is the best way to insure opportunities to connect and talk. If we are not careful, we will allow our schedules to overwhelm us so that we never take the time to create a relaxed environment that fosters conversation.

Don't get angry if they don't seem like they want to talk to you. That is perfectly normal. Especially as your children grow into their teenage years they will at times seem distant and unresponsive. Having had three teenagers of my own, I can tell you that sometimes you feel great if you get just a grunt! Don't give up hope. If you are being patient and loving in your communication, they are hiding away more in their hearts than you think they are.

You will want to put energy and thought into the kind of environments that you create. Make sure your family spends some time around a meal. Set boundaries on the amount of time they spend watching television, playing video games and doing whatever young people do on their computers. I am a big believer in getting them physically active. Exercise will improve their moods and will make them easier to connect with. (As a side note, if you as a parent are not getting enough exercise, maybe it's *your* mood that needs improvement … but again I digress.)

I have a friend from college who is the pastor of a growing church in Florida. One day, when his son was five years old, my friend was mowing his lawn. As is typical of many men, he employs a variety of tools to get the job done: lawn mowers, rakes, blowers, edgers and an assortment of trimming tools. His son loved to "help" although he was not old enough to do the job effectively. If you are the lawn maintenance spouse, you know from experience that children "helping" are usually more trouble than anything else. Nevertheless, my friend pointed out to his son all of the grass clippings that were on the driveway and told him that he could help by "blowing off the grass." Gleefully, the child accepted the mission and took off with the adorable confidence of a little boy pretending to be a man. Much to his surprise, as my friend came around on the next lap, he saw his son on his knees huffing and puffing, trying to blow the grass off the driveway with his mouth! You laugh, but he's a lot like us – even though he had power tools available to him, he failed to plug into the power source. Because he had not used the available tools, he ended up frustrated, burned out and totally ineffective.

Patience is one of the "power tools" God has given us to make us effective parents. We must plug into His Spirit for the power to raise our children right. Remember, *good parenting grows from a relationship with God.* When I plug into His love it will produce the kind of patience I need to communicate effectively with my child – even during their teenage years. Remember that lots of other people have traveled this path before you. You can do this with God's help.

Remember Your Kindness

Love is kind as well as patient. Kindness goes a long way in communicating with adults and children. Sometimes it is hard to be kind when your nerves are frazzled and you are on the edge, but the dividends are worth the sacrifice. Be careful not to confuse kindness with weakness, a lack of authority or enabling your children when they disobey. Be kind, but maintain your authority in their lives.

When I was in second grade I fell in love with my teacher, Miss Vaughn. She exercised kindness with authority in one particular occasion that I will never forget. She was totally unlike my first grade teacher, Mrs. Folger, who wore a beehive hairdo and could put the fear of God into a Marine drill sergeant. Miss Vaughn was young and pretty and nice, and I told her on one occasion that I was going to marry her.

In Miss Vaughn's class we had what we called "reading circle." This was where we all sat in a circle and each of us would stand up and read in front of the entire class out loud. I am not sure who came up with this particular form of torture, but for some of the children it was incredibly painful and embarrassing. The boy who sat next to me struggled with reading. In fact, one day he had to have help on nearly every word. You can imagine how embarrassing it must have been for him to be humiliated like that. When he had been sufficiently embarrassed by his attempt at reading, Miss Vaughn mercifully told him to sit down. To demonstrate my own gift of mercy, I pulled his chair from under him and he hit the floor with a thud. Everybody in the class laughed. The boy began to cry and Miss Vaughn, without ever raising her voice or losing her composure, told me to go to the principal's office. I immediately called the engagement off because I knew she was going to be way too high maintenance. It was not until much later in life that I appreciated the power of her communication style — always kind but always authoritative.

"Greener Grass" Is Usually Over a Sewer

In loving communication, there is no room for jealousy. I am always amazed at the way we are tempted to compare ourselves against others — and aren't afraid to communicate those comparisons to our kids. The comparison game never leads to a good outcome. Whenever we compare jobs, spouses, talents or the so-called "success" of our children we always come out losers. This can lead to the "greener grass" syndrome and will make us ineffective. God has given you children that are as individual and unique as their own fingerprints. Stop trying to compare your situation to others. Trying to motivate your kids by negative comparisons rarely leads to constructive behavior.

Truthfully, we have no idea what other's situations are like anyway. Have you ever found yourself getting jealous of someone because they seem to have it all together? You know what I am talking about. You have felt like ramming the minivan with the bumper sticker bragging about the honor student inside. I saw a funny bumper sticker once that summed it up pretty well: *My child can beat up your honor student.*

Playing the comparison game can be destructive, so don't do it. It will lead you to adopt a parenting style that makes you more concerned about what others think about you as a parent than what is best for your child. I have seen many parents fall into this rhythm, and breaking cadence with it is very difficult. Communicate and make decisions based on what is best for your child and forget about what others may think. They have not been given the responsibility — or the gifts necessary — to raise your child. God gave those to you.

Never Give Up

To you parents who are struggling to communicate effectively with your child I want to offer an encouraging word. Don't ever give up. When it comes to communicating with teenagers, sometimes you just need to *persevere*, as the writer of First Corinthians tells us. The primary parenting advice that I can give to parents of teens is to hang on because better days are coming. I have been in ministry long enough to know that the craziness of the teenage years is not necessarily indicative of what the final product will look like. We all need to thank God for that!

Several years ago I was snow skiing with a pastor friend of mine named Paul. As a teenager, Paul hated his father and went through a very difficult time with his parents. His parents were Christians who were totally involved in church, read the Bible and did all the things they were supposed to do in order to have a Christian home. They were not perfect, but they tried to follow God's instructions. You can imagine how it must have torn their hearts out to have such conflict between them and their son, especially when he said things like "I hate you." Paul became so rebellious that he experimented with drugs and alcohol and even ran away from home. Sitting on a curb one sunny afternoon, hurt, separated from his family and running from God, he asked a passerby what time it was. The man stopped and looked at his disheveled appearance and said, "Son, it is time to get right with God."

Fast forward twenty years. I am sitting in a car with Paul, who is now the pastor of a growing church in New England. We have spent most of the day skiing and talking about what God has been doing in our lives. His mom and dad – the ones he declared he hated twenty years earlier – are in town for a visit. They are so proud of him. Paul's dad walks out of the house and starts approaching the car. In mid-sentence Paul jumps out and runs to his side and holds his dad's arm as they cross the treacherous ice on the driveway.

For just a moment I feel warm all over. It is cold outside but I feel like I am witnessing one of the great moments that every parent needs to experience. It is a moment of hope. I look at my friend and imagine that this scene probably seemed impossible to his parents at one time. I am sure that when their son ran away from home as a teenager they never thought that he would direct such respect and love toward them. But at that moment I am a witness to the power of patience and kindness.

I pray I never forget that day in the mountains of New England. God infused my soul with hope that day. No matter how difficult the road may seem with your kids, never quit and never give up. Things will get better, and probably sooner than you think. You will look back one day and laugh about all the things you went through. And one day, when your children have children of their own, you will smile. At that time, you will be the one to remind them that there is hope.

Chapter SIX
Stop Kidding Around:
Communicating with Authority

I like tools. It does not really matter what kind because tools are cool. I don't always like doing the work, but I feel manly by simply owning lots of tools. Among the many that I own is an assortment of hammers. As I am not a carpenter, I'm not really sure why I have so many, but I do. Evidently this damaged gene has been passed on to our son.

When Brandon was four he went through a stage of driving nails into everything he could find. He drove nails into the dirt. He nailed them into his bedroom walls. He would try to nail objects into the floor. He would hammer on every conceivable thing you could think of. We tried everything to keep him from hammering nails into valuable things like furniture and cats. We set up boundaries and even had designated areas where he could lawfully nail stuff. I remember coming home from work one day to find nails in our living room coffee table.

One day Brandon discovered that I had a rubber hammer. If you have any experience with tools, you know that a rubber hammer has a very specific purpose. It is used to tap things that a regular hammer would damage. It definitely was not made to hammer nails. Before long I found Brandon nailing nails to his little heart's content with my rubber hammer. After I took it from him I could see the scars. It had been abused because it was not used for the right purpose.

If you are going to communicate with your children effectively and with authority, you have to understand the purpose of your communication. The truth is, we communicate for many reasons. We instruct, we warn, we lead, we learn, we express love and we assert our authority. We also point our children to Jesus Christ like a warrior with an arrow. In fact, one of the primary reasons we communicate with our children is found in what the Apostle Paul wrote to the church at Ephesus: *"When you talk, do not say harmful things, but say what people need — words that will help others become stronger. Then what you say will do good to those who listen to you"* (Ephesians 4:29). In other words, our words should help our children grow stronger.

Be Clear

If you are going to communicate with authority, you must be clear. When my wife and I communicate, being clear with each other is essential. Kim decided long ago that one of the qualifications of a good husband – one who loves his wife like Christ loved the church – is that he takes out the trash. She also thinks that a good husband should *never have to be asked* to take out the trash. Before we came to understand one another, she would sigh and say things like, "I wish someone would take out this trash." I agreed with her. I wished someone would take it out, too. Because my "dumb husband" brain hears only what it wants to hear, I have to be spoken to clearly. Kim has since learned to be clear and asks me to take out the trash directly. I always agree and then with a cheerful attitude tell one of our kids to do it. If I, as an experienced adult, have to be spoken to clearly, you can bet that your little rug rats need clear communication even more. They haven't even developed "selective hearing" yet.

If you are not clear it can end up being rather funny. Once I took my family to a giant aquarium. The experience was wonderful; however, the fine print on the tickets made me wonder about the people running that place. Did they even understand what they were communicating? The admission tickets went through all the "dos and don'ts" to make your visit a good one. It told you what you could expect at check-in and what time the aquarium closed. Precisely what you would expect to find.

Then, it stated what NOT to bring. This is where it got confusing to me. The first item on the fine print said, "*No guns.*" I understand that. This is an aquarium, not a safari. But I am not sure if they said this to prevent gang violence or if they were afraid that Bubba might be tempted to bring home some supper.

Next you were instructed not to bring *knives*. Again, good rule. Can't be too careful. Then it said, "*No lighters or matches.*" I am not sure if they were trying to prevent people from smoking in public, from burning their trash in public, or if they thought some redneck might be tempted to start a fish fry. Still, I get why you would put all of this on the ticket. It's just the last one that made me wonder what in the world they were thinking.

The last item was, "*NO FISHING POLES.*" Are you serious? No fishing poles at a giant aquarium with whales and sharks? I grew up in the South, where people love them a good fishing hole, but *no fishing poles*? Are there really people out there who expect to go fishing at the whale exhibit? Sometimes you can be clear ... and clearly ridiculous. I think you get my point – you have to be clear when you communicate if you want your words to be powerful and authoritative.

Be Consistent

If you want to establish a tone of authority with your children, you have to be consistent. Parents who make threats but then never follow through undermine their own authority. If you say that you are going to punish a child for a certain behavior, do not let the behavior go unpunished. Your child will learn very quickly who "runs the show." You have to follow through every time until obedience becomes the normal response.

Presenting a unified front to your children is also important. Children are very adept at pitting one parent against the other. When you allow them to do that, you allow them to undermine your authority. Parents have to back each other up. Let your children know right away that what one parent says goes for the other as well. Not backing a decision by your spouse will lead to a child-centered home where the parents are at the mercy of the scheming of their children. God never intended for homes to be run that way and it always causes problems with discipline.

Being consistently united can be challenging if you are divorced and your children spend part of the time with their other parent. It is important to have a conversation about the need for consistency. If the other parent disagrees or refuses to cooperate, which is too often the case, then you have to let your child know that you expect them to follow your rules when they are with you. Do not let threats of moving in with the other parent or comparisons of how much more fun it is at the other house dissuade you from staying consistent with God's principles. It may be hard to stick to your guns, but it always is best for the child.

Command Rather Than Demand

Some parents can get frustrated with their children. Let me rephrase that. *All* parents get frustrated with their children because, well, children can be frustrating. When you are frustrated you will tend to try and make demands for respect rather than commanding respect with your attitude and actions. When you give the "I-am-your-mom-so-you-had-better-listen" speech or the "you-had-better-do-it-because-I-said-so" talk – even though that is technically true – you are coming across as demanding obedience rather than commanding respect. It is much better to maintain control. Most of the time, obedience comes with respect, not the other way around. When you are calm, consistent and matter-of-fact about your decisions, it creates a much better environment for communication and things will be much more pleasant around your house.

Don't Say Harmful Things

In Ephesians 4:29 Paul instructs us to avoid saying "harmful things." Saying harmful things is easy when we are angry or when we are caught up in the moment. Now you've probably figured out that I am not one who thinks that children are so fragile that you have to walk around on eggshells as a parent. I am not suggesting that my parents never raised their voice at me or never got frustrated with me. In fact, this may come as a shock to you, but I was not a perfect child. Are you kidding me? I was a nightmare at times. It is a miracle that my parents are still sane today. I think the only thing that got them through was the hope that one day I would have kids of my own and would receive payment in full. As they say, payback is a monster. Well, that is not technically what they say, but this is a Christian book. You get the idea I am sure.

I remember making my mom so angry once that she sent me outside to get a "switch" so she could spank me. Yes, my parents spanked me, but not nearly as much as I deserved. And, no, I am not bitter or warped, nor do I hate them. If you grew up in the South you know what a "switch" is. It is not something that turns on the light, or a change of direction, but rather a small, flexible branch from a tree that is not much bigger than a twig. When you get a spanking with a switch it stings but it does not do any damage to your hindquarters.

So my mom sends me out to get my *own switch* so she could spank me! With all the sincerity I can muster, I bring back a twig about six inches long. Her face turns red, steam starts erupting from her ears, her nostrils flare and she tells me to go back out and get something "more appropriate" or it would be even worse for me. So, being the obedient and thoughtful person that I am, I grab my dad's ax, go to the woods and chop down a small tree about twelve feet tall and drag it into the house. When my mom sees it she turns her head and tries to hide the fact that she is laughing. Finally she cannot contain it any longer. She bursts out into sidesplitting laughter. There was no spanking for me that afternoon.

I tell you that story to illustrate a simple point. My mom, saint that she was for putting up with me, never said harmful things to me. I am not suggesting that she never got angry or never punished me. I am saying that I never recall her calling me stupid or saying that she wished I had not been born or that I would never amount to anything. Those things should never be said to a child. Those impressionable little minds will remember it years down the road.

On the other hand, as Paul said, we should try to say things that will make our children stronger. Words of affirmation, love, encouragement and blessing should be given generously. Sometimes words of correction are necessary, but never words of hate or bitterness that can poison who our children will become.

Be An Encourager

You have probably experienced parents who take the building of their child's self-esteem way too far in the wrong direction. They make the mistake of praising talent or looks rather than character and hard work. Other parents do their children a disservice by lowering the bar so drastically that they place little responsibility and few consequences on their kids' shoulders. Those children will be damaged in the long run because they will be shocked when they discover that no one gives out "participation ribbons" in the competitive atmosphere of the real world.

With that said, I think you should be the biggest encourager of your child. Praise character and hard work. Let them know how much you love them every day. Let them know that you are proud of them. Try your best to be positive and help them see the rewards that come from working hard and doing right.

My mother believed in being an encourager. In fact, she may have taken it too far sometimes. During my freshman year, I made the varsity track team at the small high school where I attended in North Carolina. I ended up being a pretty good runner that year, competing in the state championship race for the mile run. I will never forget it. I had worked really hard that year and now I had the chance to be the very best in the state if I could just beat everyone else in our classification.

The starting gun was fired and we were off and running. The fans were cheering from the stands but I could just make out my mom's voice above the rest of the crowd. As we came around the last turn of the last lap I was leading the race by a pretty good margin and it looked like I was going to win the state championship. About 70 yards from the finish line, I heard my mom's voice much louder than I had on the previous laps. I looked to my left and realized why. With the embarrassment that only a teenager can feel, I discovered that my mom had left the stands and somehow had made it onto the inside field of the track. She was yelling and cheering me on...and running beside me step for step. I could not believe it – I was going to beat everybody to the finish line except my mom.

Maybe you should refrain from being *that* big of an encourager, but definitely cheer on your kids.

Conversation Killers

You need all the help you can get when it comes to conversing with your kids. So be careful not to sabotage your communication by being guilty of these common conversation killers. These will especially kill conversation with teenagers.

1. **Trying to force conversation.** This is a tactic that makes you feel like you're making an effort, but rarely works. It will not work with your child, your teen or your spouse. Conversation will flow when it comes out of the natural setting. You must spend significant time together for this to happen. Here's a thought – don't wait until they are teenagers to get in the "habit" of frequent and transparent communication.

2. **Belittling the problem.** Parents are often guilty of saying things that belittle the problems their children are facing. Making comments about them not being in the real world, or that their attraction is just puppy love, or that if they think their problems are big now just wait until they have to start supporting a family, do not help. Their problems are real to them. Just remember that teenagers are very emotional and things that seem very small to you can seem like the end of the world to them.

3. **Negative conversation.** Always being negative will erode your credibility with your children and destroy any opportunity you have to engage in meaningful conversation. Constant negativity can turn a child into a terminally negative adult.

4. **Judgmental tones and body language.** We often communicate more with our body language than with the words we actually say. Be aware of judgmental tones and negative body language – such as hands on hips – when speaking to your children. Many people seem to remember their parents communicating to them in that way but are oblivious to the fact that they do the same thing to their own kids.

5. **Unfair generalizations.** Phrases like "you always" or "you never" are unfair generalizations. Normally, those statements are untrue and they almost always shut down any openness to change that may have been there to begin with. Also, avoid gross exaggerations as much as possible. "I have told you a million times" is false and tends to throw

obstacles into the path of the conversation. On the other hand, lots of focused attention and steady eye contact can open the door to communication. It says I am interested in you and you are important to me.

6. **An unforgiving spirit.** Bringing up the past is a constant temptation when trying to make a point with your child. Many parents hold onto grudges and hurts from their past, so it is hard for them to let things go. You have to be willing to forgive. I am not suggesting that you ignore a child's past behaviors or irresponsibility. If your teenage daughter gets six speeding tickets in a one-year span and you refuse to let her drive to the beach with her friends, that is not being unforgiving, that is being a responsible parent. On the other hand, constantly nagging her about it every time she leaves for school can cause major damage to your relationship. Forgive and then leave things in the past.

Effective pastor that I am, I give my wife and kids plenty of opportunities to practice their forgiveness skills. Kim and I had been married for about a year when we bought our first house. One day I got home early and pulled my car into the garage and shut the door behind me. Usually, I left the garage door open and since she did not have a garage door opener in her car, she did not think I was home when she arrived a few minutes after me. Being the fun guy that I am, I hid in the closet in our bedroom waiting for her. It took several minutes. I could hear her walking around the house taking care of her business. Finally, she came into the bedroom and opened her closet. When she did, I grabbed her and screamed. I won't tell you the rest of the story. Suffice it to say, that was not the smartest thing I ever did. I was in the doghouse for quite a while. But it did give her a chance to work on that forgiving spirit the Bible talks about.

Forgiveness is not always easy and sometimes you really have to work on having a forgiving spirit with your kids. Or your husband. Just ask Kim. She still does not like closets.

CHAPTER SEVEN
Who's Misbehaving?
How to Model Behavior for Your Children

William Bennett, author of The Book of Virtues, says, "For children to take morality seriously, they must be in the presence of adults who take morality seriously."[4] I think one of the main reasons we see behavior problems in our children, besides the fact that they have a sin nature, is quite simple – they watch how we live. If we want our children to live with integrity we must model that behavior in our daily lives. We can't say, "Do what I say and not what I do." That simply does not work.

A number of years ago, when our daughter Brooke was three years old, I learned again the importance of modeling behavior. Kim and I and our three children were driving to the church for a special event. In a hurry, of course. Why is it that when you are in a hurry the *slowest* people get in front of you? I am not a very patient person at the best of times, and even less when I'm in a hurry. Kim had spoken to me on several occasions about the way I had been

---

[4] Bennett, William, The Book of Virtues: A Treasury of Great Moral Stories (New York: Simon and Schuster, 1993),
p. 225.

acting when I got behind the wheel. She said that I was getting worse and she was afraid the kids were starting to pick up on it.

Since we were headed to church, and I was the pastor, I thought maybe I would try to heed Kim's advice for once. I was patiently waiting on the person in front of me, even though I felt like ramming my bumper into her car. The person driving the car fit every stereotype I could think of – she was an elderly lady whose head was barely visible over the seat and she had her left blinker on but she was not turning. I was so proud of myself for holding my tongue and not losing my temper. This was a moment to savor, a sign of real spiritual growth; indeed, it was no less than evidence of the fact that I was truly a model dad.

My illusion was shattered when Brooke leaned up in her car seat and yelled at the top of her sweet little voice, "Move it, fool!" I quickly scolded her for talking like her mom, but I wasn't fooling anybody. It was an eye-opener for me. My kids were not watching me as a pastor who stood in front of lots of people and gave grand sermons. They saw me in my every day, real world setting and no amount of "God-talk" could hide the real me.

Moses gave a perfect plan for modeling the right behavior to our children in Deuteronomy 6. We looked at some of these verses in an earlier chapter but I would like for you to see them again. I love the way this passage reads in *The Message* paraphrase.

> *Write these commandments that I've given you today on your hearts. Get them inside of you and then get them inside your children. Talk about them wherever you are, sitting at home or walking in the street; talk about them from the time you get up in the morning to when you fall into bed at night. Tie them on your hands and foreheads as a reminder; inscribe them on the doorposts of your homes and on your city gates (Deuteronomy 6:6-9 The Message).*

In this passage we see three important keys to modeling Godly behavior: authenticity, tenacity, and transparency.

Be Authentic

Being authentic is critical because your children are going to follow your example. Moses writes that God's people must have God's commands and instructions *on their heart*. This does not mean that you have to have the whole Bible memorized, but that you have to take it seriously and live out the Christian life from your core. You do not have to be *perfect* but you do have to be *real*. When a person is real and authentic, their message comes across loud and clear even though they occasionally fail or fall short.

I love authentic, real people. They speak volumes into my life. I have a cousin named Raleigh. He is different. He is filled with the kind of purity and love that changes people around him. He is in his forties but he still lives at home with his mom and dad. You see, Raleigh had a difficult time being born. His brain was severely damaged during the birthing process and as a result, he has never been able to walk and has the mental capacity of a four-year-old child.

The doctors told his parents that he probably would not live past the age of five, but he is still alive and doling out loads of God's truth with his simple life. He still goes to a school designed for people just like him. In my opinion, the people who work with Raleigh and his friends are champions for their selfless work and commitment. But don't think for a minute that working with Raleigh does not have its rewards. He has a wonderful personality and is one of the funniest people I have ever met. Sometimes, God ordains people like Raleigh to teach us what it means to be real.

Not long ago some of the people connected to his school decided to do a fundraising event. Part of the event included a "southern gospel" musical act. The problem was that Raleigh, evidently, does not like southern gospel music. The auditorium was packed with the students, their families and friends of the school. Everybody was dressed up and on their best behavior. Just a few seconds after they began to sing Raleigh started yelling, "Booooo!" The more they sang the louder he shouted. His mother was mortified and told him that he had to say "Yeah" because they were trying to help his school. So Raleigh started yelling, "Yeah...Booo! Yeah...Booo!" Raleigh loves to keep it real.

When I first heard that story I was rather jealous. I would love to be able to yell "Booo!" to the things I do not like. Bad service in a restaurant? Booo! Fake people in churches? Booo! Horrible customer service in a department store? Just start pointing and yelling "Booo!" I think that would be one of the greatest things ever.

I don't want you to miss the point that Raleigh taught me. I wonder if God ever feels like yelling *"Yeah...Booo!"* at me. *"Yeah, you are my child." "Booo, for your behavior." "Yeah, you are my church." "Booo, for arguing over silly things like musical styles, Bible translations, denominational labels and clothing styles while people all around are dying and going to hell." "Yeah, you will spend eternity with me." "Booo, for not living out my purpose so that others can come with you." "Yeah, your heart has been changed." "Booo, your actions don't always match your heart."*

I know that I can't fool God with my life. He knows if I am authentic or not. The scary thing is that I can't even fool my kids. They know, too, just from watching my life.

Be Tenacious

Moses tells us that we have to do whatever it takes to implant God's commands inside of us and our children. The Hebrew word that is used here gives the idea of sharpening again and again so that you keep an edge. That is what we must do with or children. We must teach and live with such tenacity that the edges on our children's lives are constantly honed. This goes hand in hand with the idea that we explored in chapter two from Psalm 127: parents are like warriors and our children are like arrows. We have to be relentless in pointing the arrow to the target so that its purpose can be accomplished.

Sometimes parenting can seem really hard, but it does not have to be as hard as we make it. Keep in mind that our job is a marathon not a sprint. You will not win every battle, but with God's help and a lot of tenacity, you will win the war. Our job is not to create children in our own image, but rather to get God's word into their lives so that they will become what He wants. They are not going to do everything that you or I like. They will even make choices that we do not care for. Our job is to get them to the target so they can be what God wants them to be.

Be Transparent

Moses goes on to say that the best way to teach our children these values is in the normal rhythm of life. We tend to think that the most valuable teaching comes from sitting in church listening to the sermon or in the children's ministry. On the contrary, the best teaching rarely comes from the "sit still while I instill" method, but from the "let's lie on our backs in the backyard and stare at the stars" method.

What God is saying is that we have more and better teaching moments in the normal course of everyday living than in all of the hours in church combined. Am I suggesting that going to church is unimportant? Of course not. I am a pastor, for goodness sake! What God is saying is that His word only becomes truly relevant when we model it in the course of normal living. When we get up and get ready for school we teach. When we play ball we teach. When we eat supper we teach. The Scripture is saying that, while church is important, the ride to church may be even more important when it comes to what our kids learn.

As I look back on it, a lot of lessons in our house have been taught on the way to church. One Sunday morning Brandon and I were on our way to church in one car while Kim, Brittney and Brooke were riding in another car. It was just us boys hanging out. Brandon was being kind of quiet and so was I. Two dudes can do that without anyone thinking that someone is mad.

Suddenly Brandon blurted out, "Why do they hate God, Dad?" I was flabbergasted. I had no idea what he was talking about. "Why does who hate God?" I asked. "All these people whose cars are still in their driveway," he said. "They are not going to church so they must hate God, huh, Dad?" In that quiet moment on the way to church I had an opportunity to teach my son about what it really means to love God. It is in those moments of transparency during the normal course of daily living that we communicate the most to our children.

Just what are you teaching?

Chapter EIGHT
The Key to Happy Kids and Peaceful Parents

Very few subjects cause more controversy and disagreement than the subject of disciplining children. Most of us want to think we get it right and that our opinions and philosophy are correct. If we are honest, however, most of us would admit that we don't have it all together and that we really need help in getting our children to behave. The right kind of discipline is necessary for raising happy, well-adjusted kids and for keeping a peaceful environment in the home. Proverbs 29:17 says, *"Discipline your children, and they will give you happiness and peace of mind."* The big question is how do you discipline effectively and keep your sanity as a parent?

I go back to my assertion that parenting does not have to be as hard as we make it out to be sometimes. You can maintain discipline and help your children become responsible and respectful by following God's plan. When you follow His principles you will find that you can raise godly children without losing your mind. This even applies if you have an appropriately labeled "strong-willed" child.

To a strong-willed child, the words "no" and "don't" are just theories. Throughout this book I have shared personal stories with you about our children. These stories are meant to help you identify with the values I am teaching. You have probably noticed that I tell more stories about our son, Brandon, than I do about our daughters, Brittney and Brooke. That's because

Kim and I have had a lot more "opportunities" to test these biblical principles on him. He was our "strong-willed" child. I am not picking on him. He simply gave us more scenarios that make good illustrations — as those of you who have a relentless child with fathomless depths of energy will understand.

For those of you who have compliant, easygoing children, don't get too cocky. When Brittney, our oldest, was born we thought we were the best parents ever. To be honest, I was kind of proud. I considered myself a role model for parents who wanted to know how to have a child who behaved in public.

Then Brandon was born. After a few months, I withdrew my name from consideration for early induction into the parenting hall of fame. Form the time he could walk and talk that boy could find mischief faster than any human I have ever known. He was clever, too. I remember once when he was around three he had gotten into trouble on a Sunday morning before church. He was already in trouble because had taken a magic marker and marked up the seats in our new minivan. When we got to church I noticed that he had stolen all the change out of the coin holder as well. When I confronted him about his toddler felony he never even missed a beat. Without hesitation he said, "I got them for Jesus, Daddy." I barely kept my composure. It is one thing to have a little demon, but when your fallen angel can outsmart you then you have a real challenge on your hands.

So what is a parent to do about discipline? Here are several time-honored, biblically accurate principles that will put consistent discipline within your reach.

Draw Clear Lines

One of the biggest causes of frustration for parents is actually of their own making. When you are inconsistent and fail to draw clear lines, problems always ensue. You have to let your child know the rules and the consequences up front. I have seen parents let their children get away with direct disobedience because they thought that it was cute and then punish the child for accidentally spilling their milk. Can you see the problem? Punishing childish behavior while letting willful defiance slide creates problems for your child. She does not know what to expect. Because she will not know where the lines are drawn, she will push the envelope even farther. Clear lines and consistent discipline help a child become responsible and mature. Solomon said, "A child is going to do foolish things. But correcting him will drive his foolishness far away from him" (Proverbs 22:15, NIRV).

My father was very good at establishing clear lines and communicating the consequences for wrong behavior. He normally did not yell or lose his cool with me. He was very matter-of-fact when it came to disciplining me. This helped me to know that he was strict but fair.

When I was a senior in high school, I had a set curfew for weeknights and another for weekend nights. On special occasions I could get permission to stay out past curfew, but I knew what time I had to be home. I started developing a habit of coming in a few minutes after curfew. It was not blatant; I was not getting home a couple of *days* late, just a few minutes. It started with being three minutes late and evolved into being fifteen to thirty minutes late. My dad had a reminder meeting with me. He told me that I was to be home "at or before" curfew and if I came in late again I would not be allowed into the house. Since I was only a few months away from graduating high school, I did not take him too seriously. After all, I considered myself a man.

The very next night I went out on a date with my girlfriend. I knew exactly how much time it took to get home and so I was squeezing out every possible moment with her. I left with the precise amount of time necessary to walk through the door with about five seconds to spare. Of course, I had not planned on getting stuck behind the world's oldest and slowest driver. I would have passed her but my 1973 Pinto station wagon needed a sizable head start to get up enough speed to pass a horse and buggy. When I was finally able to get around her, the race was on. I slid into the driveway and was out of my car almost before it stopped rolling. When I got to the door I was about sixty seconds late. I felt certain that my dad would extend some grace because I had really tried.

He met me at the door with a smile and asked how my date was. He asked if I had a good time. Then he said "good night" and with that, I started to make my way through the door into the living room. My dad stopped me, and with a puzzled look on his face, asked me where I was going. I informed him that I was going to my bedroom. He smiled and said, "No you are not. You were late. I realize you were only a minute late, but you were still late. You should have planned better. Next time, when I tell you to be home at a certain time, make sure that you are not late. Now you have a good night. I love you and I will see you in the morning. By the way, if you try to sneak in during the night you will really be in trouble." With that, he smiled and locked the door behind him.

I could not believe it! I headed back down the steps to spend the night in my 1973 Pinto station wagon. After a few minutes I came to my senses and drove to my grandma's house and spent the night in her spare bedroom. I will never forget the lesson that my dad taught me that night. He drew clear lines and enforced them. I am confident that I became a better person that night because my dad loved me enough to be tough.

Draw the Lines in the Right Places

I also think it is important to know *where* to draw the line. Many parents cause themselves unnecessary grief because they simply draw the lines in the wrong places. Not every battle is worth fighting, especially with teenagers. Kim and I decided early on that we would enforce certain moral and behavioral guidelines that were absolute. There is no wiggle room in these guidelines and we will fight those battles.

Everything else is fair game. Some things are not worth the battle. So what if they do not like the same hairstyles, music styles or clothing styles as we do? I am not going to fight over things that really make no difference. We have tried to make sure our children hold deep moral, biblical and spiritual standards. These principles are rock-solid and unmovable and are based on Scripture, not on our personal preferences. We draw as few lines as possible on everything else. Producing respect and responsibility is our main goal for our children. If you take this approach you have to remain consistent in your discipline and clear as you communicate to your children about risks, rewards and responsibilities.

A number of years ago we bought a trampoline for our kids. It was a big hit around our house. At the time Brittney was thirteen, Brandon was twelve and Brooke was five. They had hours of fun on it. One day I heard my wife, Kim, yell out, "Ritchie, come here now!" I was pretty sure that I had not done anything worth being yelled at, so I assumed one of the kids was up to something. I went into the back yard to see Kim glaring up at something on our roof. I turned around and discovered that Brandon was on the roof of our house with a giant grin on his face. He had set up the trampoline about halfway between the house and the pool and was getting ready to jump from the roof, onto the trampoline, and – if his physics were correct – into the deep end of the pool.

Kim was looking at me with a mixture of terror, anger and warning in her eyes and said, "You had better tell your son..." (I am not sure why he is referred to as "my son" only when he is acting up) "...that he had better not jump or he is in big trouble." When I looked up at Brandon, two things became crystal clear to me: first, he would not jump if I told him he could not; and second, he would *definitely* jump the first opportunity he got when we were not around. So, being a practitioner of teaching my kids about risks, rewards and responsibilities, I looked at Brandon and told him to go ahead and jump. I thought Kim was going to put the smack down on me. I explained to her that she might be able to keep Brandon from jumping temporarily, but that he definitely would jump when we were not there. If he fell and broke something while we were there, at least we could take him to the hospital. Knowing her son, she reluctantly agreed. He jumped. No bones were broken. Everybody survived. Kim and I stayed consistent (and married) because we had maintained a unified front.

Being consistent and drawing clear lines also means that you must follow through and do what you say. If you tell the child that you are going to punish him for a certain behavior, then do what you said. The Bible says that if you are not consistent in this area, you do not truly love your child! *"If you refuse to discipline your children, it proves you don't love them; if you love your children, you will be prompt to discipline them"* (Proverbs 13:24). Being consistent also means not resorting to bribing and not caving in to their complaining.

Start Early

The writer of Proverbs says, *"Discipline your children while they are young enough to learn. If you don't, you are helping them to destroy themselves"*

(Proverbs 19:18, GNT). Many parents make the mistake of waiting too long before they begin disciplining their children. I do not claim to be an expert in cognitive development for children, nor am I trying to set a date that's right for everybody to begin corporal punishment. I am simply saying that you must start correcting poor behavior early or habits will begin to develop in your child that will be difficult to disengage later. Each child is different and your approach to discipline will be different for each child. The one factor that should be the same in every case is starting early.

Little tantrums that look so cute at an early age get ugly in a hurry. Somebody has to be in charge and if you give that right up early on, it's difficult to win back. You have to remember to operate from your position of authority so that you command attention and obedience. If you do not, you will be controlled by your child and will have a child-run household. This is a position of weakness and is damaging to the long-term wellbeing of your family and your child.

Instill Respect and Responsibility

After pointing your children to the target of a relationship to Christ, I believe the next main responsibility of parenting is to instill *responsibility* and *respect* into your children. I have observed over many years of ministry that children who learn those two things normally turn out to be the kind of adults that their parents were hoping for. I am not saying that they will be perfect, but I really believe if they are taught to be respectful and responsible they will have a much greater chance of fulfilling their God-given destiny in the long run.

Respect and responsibility go hand-in-hand. The more responsibility you can give your child for his or her own choices, the more character he or she will develop. I believe that responsibility should come first, then privilege. Because we love our children, we love giving them things. Generosity toward our kids is a good thing, but if we are not careful, we will give too much privilege without any responsibility. Give responsibility first, then let privilege follow.

One way for children to learn responsibility is by taking part in the functioning of your household. Assigning chores and jobs should be a part of every child's training. With all three of our children we have assigned tasks that they have to perform, like household chores, cleaning their rooms, doing the dishes and mowing the lawn. In addition, once they reach a certain age, they are responsible for their own laundry and managing their own money.

I am sure my children are not the only ones to complain. We have heard complaints about shoes, clothes, electronic gadgets and even school lunches. Maybe you, too, have felt like nothing was ever quite good enough. We made a policy change a couple of years ago that has virtually put a stop to the complaining. We decided that once our children reached ninth grade they were going to be responsible for their own money – and their own "stuff."

This is how we did it. Kim and I averaged out what we spent on each of our children in a year's time on clothing, entertainment, school lunches, toiletries, haircuts and other essentials, and divided that number by twelve. We opened a checking account and a savings account for each of them. At the beginning of every month we deposit one month's living expenses into their accounts.

We have three rules: 1) You must tithe, 2) you must save, and 3) if you run out of money before the beginning of the next month, we don't care. If you spend all your money on movies and you have to go to school naked, that is tough. If you spend all your money on eating out with friends and you have no deodorant or toothpaste, then you probably won't have many friends to worry about anyway, so we are not giving you any more money.

This has been the greatest parenting decision we've ever made. I never hear a complaint about taking a lunch to school any more. I have been informed that school lunches cost money (who knew?) and that a lunch that Mom fixes is free (to them) so how dare I suggest that they just buy their own lunch whenever they are running late! Making someone responsible for her own life is an amazing and beautiful thing. I have not even had to make the "just wait until you get in the real world" speech in a long time.

I truly believe healthy self-esteem comes from giving children responsibility, because it helps them to learn the power of accomplishment. It's a good tool for us as parents, too, because it helps us develop their self-esteem the right way. Praise and positive words are important, but lessons in respect and responsibility are more important.

Avoid The Buddy System

In order to maintain discipline and gain the proper respect from your children, you must remember that you are primarily their parent, not their buddy. My job as a parent does not necessitate being my child's best friend. That does not mean that I should be cold or distant from them. It means that I should avoid trying to be like them in order to connect with them. That never works. Your children prefer friends whose birthday is close to the same century as theirs.

Children will act like you are nothing but chopped liver one minute, and like you are the greatest thing since sliced bread the next. They can't even be friends with their friends very long, for goodness sake. Stop trying to be their friend and be their parent. Be the leader. They need your leadership much more than they need to have the cool parent who dresses like them and tries to live vicariously through them. It is important that they understand who you are and where your priorities lie. Let them know that your spouse comes before them. Contrary to popular belief, they will actually be more confident and better adjusted for it. Help your child understand that he or she is not the center of your universe, but you – with God on the throne of your life – are at the center of theirs.

Be Flexible

If I have learned anything about being a parent I have learned this: you better expect the unexpected. You have to be flexible! I'm not talking about flexibility in your parenting absolutes – there must be certain parenting, moral and spiritual values that you live by. Learn to be flexible in everything else, though. You are going to need it.

Being flexible means that you must learn each of your children's unique personality type. Brittney, Brandon and Brooke are all so different that it is sometimes hard to imagine they are related to each other. What works for one child will not necessarily work for the other.

If you are going to be flexible, you must learn what type of discipline works with each child. We did not have to punish Brittney very much when she was younger. She was quiet, but we soon learned that she could be sneaky and hide things from us, so we had to adapt. We made sure that she had her own space but we also learned that just because she was compliant and quiet did not mean that she was always obedient. She was more passive-aggressive than she was defiant.

Have I mentioned that Brandon was our strong-willed child? He was fiercely independent, so we had to get his will under control. At two years old he wanted to do everything for himself. We had to learn how to navigate that. He fought just about every decision we made because he wanted to make them himself. If we got him out of his car seat he would scream and then get back into the car, get in the car seat, pull the latch down over his head, then get himself out and close the door. Every morning was a fight just to get dressed. That is, until Kim had the brilliant idea to start laying out two or three outfits that she approved of before he went to bed. He got to choose which one he wanted to wear before he went to bed. This saved hours of stress. We learned early on that spanking was not always the best alternative. He did not care – a spanking was a piece of cake to him. A much greater punishment was to make him lie on his bed for thirty minutes.

Brooke is a very affectionate person. She has a way of getting to me especially. Before she was a teenager, she would come in and sit on my lap, hug me and tell me how much she loved me. I was completely vulnerable to her manipulation! If you have one like her, you know that disciplining an affectionate child is very tough on you emotionally, but they need it just as much as the strong-willed child. You have to learn what works with each of your children.

Some Helpful Tips On Discipline

Here is some advice that will help you become a more effective disciplinarian and will help you instill character into your child.

- ## Get involved.

  Get yourself and your kids involved in a church. God never intended for you to raise your children without the help of a local church. Don't just go to church, but get involved in volunteering. In my experience, parents who share their faith and are deeply involved at church have children who stay faithful to church during their teens and twenties. Maybe it's because those children also have a much stronger Christian worldview. Deuteronomy chapter six supports this view as well.

- ## Don't compare.

  Playing the comparison game with our kids can damage them. We should never compare their accomplishments or behavior to their siblings or children from other families. We also should not play the "what if" game. What if I married that person? What if I had that job? What if my kid had that kind of talent? Comparisons lead to envy and covetousness.

- ## Say yes whenever possible.

  Kim and I decided that we would say yes as often as we could. You already have to say no to your children a lot when you are a parent. Brooke asked if she could drive my car when she was five years old. You need to say no to things that will hurt them or others. Whenever possible, however, say yes. If it does not violate your spiritual, moral or ethical code and it does not destroy their manners or their minds, think about saying yes. Who cares if they want to wear cowboy boots with shorts? Who cares if they want purple, pink and blue walls in their bedroom? Does that make a difference? No. But it could go a long way toward developing a positive atmosphere in your home.

- ## Don't be manipulated by "what everyone else is doing."

    I give you permission to use one of my favorite lines: "Not everyone is doing it, because YOU are not doing it!" Providing the necessary "push back" to their pressure will be a good example of how your kids can avoid their own peer pressure.

- ## Speak blessings over them.

    I have tried to make a habit of speaking blessings into the lives of my children. I have told each of them how I think God has gifted them, how much I think God is going to use them and how I have given them to God to serve Him with their whole life. I know that my parents did the same for me. There were times that I stopped short of doing something that would hinder my future because I remembered those words from my parents.

- ## Laugh as much as possible.

    One of the wisest men ever to live said, "People ought to enjoy every day of their lives" (Ecclesiastes 11:8, NCV). The Bible says laughter is good for us like a medicine. I am afraid that too many homes have too little laughter and fun. We need to take Jesus Christ very seriously and on everything else – we need to chill out!

    We all have days when taking this advice would help. One day I was working from home because my car was in the shop and Kim had our other car. I was in a generally grouchy mood. I had no transportation and it looked like I was not going to be able to go anywhere for a while because even my bicycle was broken. Late in the afternoon I received a phone call from Brandon's middle school. We had told him repeatedly to ride the bus home on this day because we only had one car available and no one could give him a ride. Sure enough, he had forgotten to ride the bus. To make matters worse, if someone did not pick him up in ten minutes we would be charged for after school care. I was beyond aggravated.

Suddenly I had an idea. We had one bicycle in our garage that was not being used. So I jumped on Brittney's bike – which to my delight was purple and very girly – and rode to Brandon's school. It was great! As I rode up I could overhear the middle school kids asking, with pity in their voices, whose dad was that coming to get his kid on a girl's bicycle? I pulled up to the front with great fanfare and offered Brandon a ride. He accepted, jumped on the handlebars, and we rode off together, father and son, on a girl's bike. We still laugh about that today. Sometimes, you just have to laugh instead of getting mad.

- ## Be disciplined with your discipline.

Proverbs 23:13-14 says, *"Don't fail to discipline your children. They won't die if you spank them. Physical discipline may well save them from death."* Although this goes against what some so-called "experts" teach, the Bible definitely supports the concept of corporal punishment as a part of an overall approach to discipline. It is not the only kind of discipline taught in the Bible, but Scripture clearly teaches that the appropriate use of spankings is fitting from time to time.

Spankings must be administered in the right way and at the right time to be effective. In my opinion, spankings are helpful for children from toddler age up until the later elementary school years. Spankings should be the last resort, not the first response. A spanking should never be administered in anger and you should always make the punishment fit the crime. You should never lose control! The purpose of a spanking is to discipline, not abuse.

I disagree with the thoughts of some "experts" concerning spankings or corporal punishment. In no way do I believe that a spanking, administered appropriately, leads a child to hit others. That is nonsense. On the contrary, an occasional spanking will teach a child that wrong or dangerous actions carry clear and unpleasant consequences.

Some parents choose to spank with an open hand using their palm, others choose to use an object that stings but does not bruise or harm. I believe that a spanking should be administered to a child's bottom and should never be hard enough to harm the child physically. You should never slap a child in the face or hit them with a fist. Abuse of a child is despicable and there is no room for that in any home, Christian or otherwise. Spankings should be controlled, rare and never abusive. I also believe that the parent should be very generous with eye contact, focused attention and lots of hugs so that the child does not feel alienated.

And don't forget the "this is going to hurt you more than it hurts me" speech. Just kidding – don't add insult to injury, like our parents did.

When it is over, drop it.

Colossians 3:21 says: *"Fathers, do not aggravate your children, or they will become discouraged."* It is important not to dwell on the past. Thankfully, our Heavenly Father forgives us and does not dwell on our past. When a matter is over, we must learn to drop it and leave it in the past. Bringing it up again can be tempting, but it normally that serves no good purpose.

On New Year's Day a few years ago, I was sitting in my nice comfy chair watching college football like all other men who love Jesus. Suddenly I heard a tremendous "boom" that sounded like a bomb going off. I was jolted from my state of relaxation and ran outside to discover about five or six spots of fire in my front yard. They were about three feet wide and spreading quickly. I sprinted around the back of my house in my slippers and grabbed my water hose. By the time I got back around to the front of the house — this took less than sixty seconds — my entire front yard was ablaze. I am talking *"call 911 and the fire department!"* conflagration. The fire spread so quickly that it literally burned my entire front yard and engulfed most of my neighbor's front yard. Flowerbeds, trees and grass were on fire. Nothing was spared. Fortunately, we put it out before the houses caught on fire. But it really shook me up.

It turned out that my male offspring had procured a powerful set of fireworks that only a professional is supposed to use. He thought it would be fun to set off this projectile that would be considered a weapon of mass destruction in many parts of the world. He thought it would be a good idea to set it off in our neighborhood. Where actual people live. In our driveway. In front of his girlfriend.

Since that time I have had to keep reminding myself of what the Psalmist said in Psalm 127: *"Children are a blessing from the Lord. Children are a blessing form the Lord. Children are a blessing from the Lord."* Some verses are just harder to believe than others. So far I have done a pretty good job of not bringing it up again. Putting it in a book does not count ... does it?

Chapter NINE
The 25th Hour
How to Gain More by Doing Less

According to the ancient wisdom of Solomon, smart choices and common sense are necessary ingredients for a strong household. He writes in Proverbs 24:3: "Homes are built on the foundation of wisdom and understanding." Not every choice that we make for our family is a simple matter of right and wrong. Many of the most important decisions come down to making the wisest choice. Some choices are not sinful but they are not the wisest thing to do. We often struggle with making unwise decisions, especially when it comes to schedules and activities.

In my early twenties I became the youth pastor of a large church in Florida. For one of our large group activities, we decided to take a trip to the Okefenokee Swamp in the southeastern part of Georgia. The Okefenokee Swamp is a major wetlands park and attraction that has hundreds of miles of pristine canoe and boat trails. It is a nature lover's paradise. The park is also home to many, many, many alligators.

During my spiel to the teenagers about being careful and responsible during our outing, I happened to mention the alligators only about a dozen times. I told them not to feed the alligators, not to throw things at the alligators (alligators have feelings too), not to try and swim with the alligators and not to throw their friends into the water where the alligators were lurking. After the incident, several of the boys said that it sounded like I was giving instructions for things they SHOULD do to have fun. But I am getting ahead of myself.

Everybody had a canoe except for me. I rented a small motorboat so that I could help the stragglers and those who could not paddle in a straight line keep up with the group. I think some of the girls would still be out there if I did not have that motorized boat. I kept on reminding the group that it was not a wise thing to turn over their canoe. The alligators seemed to be watching...and waiting.

On one of my excursions, I was bringing a canoe full of girls back to the group. They managed to complain about the heat, the mosquitoes, their hair, boys splashing them with water, the fact that there were no bathroom facilities and their paddles, which were obviously faulty because they kept going in circles. I was beginning to question the wisdom of planning this outing when I saw, to my astonishment, two high school boys standing with their feet on the edge of both sides of their canoe, sword-fighting with their paddles. Before I could yell out that there was a gator lying on the bank about twenty feet away, their canoe capsized and they both fell into the water.

I immediately turned to look at the giant reptile, only to see it slither into the water headed straight for the two boys and their overturned canoe. I began to panic. I did not want two of my teenagers being gator snacks, even though I was ticked at them for making such a dumb choice. After eyeballing the gator for what could not have been more than two or three seconds, I turned back to see where the boys were in the water. To my horror I saw that they were not there. That is when I realized that they both were sitting in the motorboat with me! After all these years I still have no idea how they got into the boat that quickly. I know that Jesus could walk on water and Peter gave it a shot for a few seconds but I am pretty sure that no one else has ever even tried. I guess even teenagers can learn to be like Jesus when properly motivated.

That is a funny story but I tell it to illustrate that our poor choices can have dire consequences for our families. How many times do poor scheduling choices bring negative long-term consequences? Often the choice is not between right and wrong but between the wise and the unwise. Making wise choices with your family schedule is essential for you and your children. To what activities do you say yes? To what do you say no? How much time should you allow your kids to spend in extracurricular activities? Is spending five or six nights a week chauffeuring your child to practices and games really quality family time? What does missing church because of a baseball game say to your child? Is it possible that these wholesome things are actually robbing them of their childhood? You will have to regain control of your time; otherwise good, but unwise, activities will rob you of your joy, your energy and your sense of togetherness.

In fact, Scripture tells us that we have a responsibility to ourselves and to God to make wise choices regarding our time: *"Pay careful attention, then, to how you walk—not as unwise people but as wise — making the most of the time, because the days are evil. So don't be foolish, but understand what the Lord's will is"* (Ephesians 5:15-17 HCSV).

Big Things Come First

This certainly is not groundbreaking stuff because we have all heard this before: you have to set priorities. You must figure out what the most important things are and do them first. How? By devoting enough time and attention to those priorities to make them successful. They have to come at the top of the list or they will get crowded out without your being aware of it.

You probably have heard the story about the rocks in the jar. I don't know who first told it, or what the original version is. Maybe it was a professor, a Sunday school teacher, a scientist or a marriage counselor. I have heard it in many different settings but the principle of the story is powerful. My version goes like this.

A teacher placed a jar on his desk and began to fill it with rocks. When it was filled to the brim he asked his class if the jar was full. "Yes," they responded. He then took some small pebbles and filled in the hollow spaces. "How about now?" he asked. A few said "Yes," but most, beginning to catch on, said nothing. He then filled the jar with sand and a few more thought it was completely filled up. Finally he filled it the rest of the way with water. "Is it full now?" he asked. "Yes," the students all agreed. When he asked what was the lesson, one student blurted out, "There is always room for more in your life."

The wise professor wryly responded with a twinkle in his eye, "No, the lesson is you have to put the big rocks in first or you will never get them in."

Allowing our schedule to crowd out the important things in life is so easy. We normally do not intend for that to happen. What makes it so sinister is that the activities that crowd out the most important things are normally not bad or evil. If you don't plan ahead, you will find yourself choosing between what is good and what is best, or between what is wise and what is just alright. You have to shut down the taxi service for long enough to set priorities and goals for your life, and then trim out everything that keeps you from achieving those things. You have to put the big things in first: church attendance, giving, serving, time with God and family time. Otherwise they will simply get crowded out by the good — but much less important — activities.

Operate With A Margin

Trying to fit more and more into your schedule is tempting. When we constantly add without ever subtracting anything, we deceive ourselves into thinking that we have the time and energy to get it all done and continue at a breakneck pace for a long period of time. That is not realistic. There certainly will be times when we will be busier than others. However, if we never allow any margin in our lives, we will eventually burn out or stop doing something important.

Operating with a margin means that you don't over schedule yourself or your children. Don't exhaust yourself or them by trying to do too many things. Let your children have time to be kids. A free night or two per week is okay, and doesn't mean you're passing up valuable opportunities. . You do not have to have a game, a karate lesson, a dance competition or a play date every night of the week. We can be guilty of trying to "keep up with the Jones" in more than just economics. The number of trophies on your daughter's dresser is not necessarily a good predictor of her success in life.

Sometimes learning the power of the word "No" can be a liberating experience. In fact, I believe your success will be determined by the things to which you learn to say no. Certainly we have to say yes to the important things, but we also have to learn the power of saying no to things that will rob our time and keep us from having the kind of family God intends.

I once baptized a blind woman. She was very nervous about being put under the water and she was visibly shaking when she got into the baptismal. I tried to comfort her as best I could and assured her that I would keep her from harm. When I brought her up out of the water she began to thrash around and yell as if she had been shocked. Not aware that she was just celebrating in her own way, I tried to put my arms around her to let her know that I was still there. Evidently she thought I was trying to rain on her parade – or put her back under, I don't know – but she turned to me and yelled, "Get behind me, Satan!" Sometimes you have to grit your teeth and say that to the temptation that tries to steal your priorities.

Less Is More

The Bible teaches a subtle principle that is quite freeing when you understand it, but few people get it: that is, that we can do more with less when we commit our sacrifice to God. This principle is true of the Sabbath. When I commit my time to God and give one day for the purpose of worshipping God, He promises to bless my time. I can get more done in six blessed days than I can in seven days that are not blessed. This is also true with my money. When I bring back to God the tithe – the first ten percent of my income – God promises to bless me and make my blessed 90 percent go further than my cursed 100 percent.

You can get more done in less time when you put God first. I call this the "less is more" principle. I have found this to be true in leadership as well. The fewer things I do the more I get done. When I focus, I become more like a laser and less like a flashlight. To follow the "less is more" principle in your family schedule, you may have to retrain your attitude. Once you do, however, you will never go back to the overly busy, stress-filled life without margins that characterizes many American families.

The very first time I ever traveled to the Bahamas I went to speak at a church. I knew very little about the customs of the Bahamian people, so I brought my American attitude and expectations with me. I was anxious because everyone seemed to be running late. The service was scheduled for 7:00 p.m. and no one had picked me up from my hotel. Finally, at 6:59 the pastor arrived. I thought maybe the service was already started and we would be fashionably late. When we arrived at the church around 7:15, I was shocked to see that there was no one at the church. The pastor unlocked the door and we went in. I tried to relax but I was out of my comfort zone. At 7:30, a few stragglers wandered into the auditorium, so the minister of music started playing.

I just knew that this was going to be a disaster. I had flown in from the United States and it seemed to me that they had wasted their money. I finally got up to speak at 8:00, a full hour after the service was supposed to have started. Much to my surprise the building was entirely full of people. After the service was over the pastor took me back to my hotel. He smiled and said, "Ritchie, you must put away your American watch; you are now on Bahamian time." He was telling me that I had to retrain my attitude.

Once you retrain your attitude about your schedule and your priorities, you will finally have time to stop and smell the roses – and have a heart-to-heart with your son or daughter. Try it. I promise you will like it.

CHAPTER TEN
Security Breach:
Creating a Safe Environment for Your Child

I must confess that I am a little "old school" when it comes to protecting children. I am a full-scale believer in doing whatever it takes to ensure the safety and health of my children. I was raised in a redneck culture that believed that you could get further with a kind word and a gun than just a kind word. As much as I try, I can't get all the red off of my neck, so I believe that some things are worth fighting for. Protecting your children from harm is one of those things.

My problem is that our culture has gone stark, raving mad in *overprotecting* our kids. We try to protect children from everything but, ironically, this has had the exact opposite effect that we intended. We've created a generation of young people who are completely unprepared to deal with pain and disappointment. I am not suggesting that you treat your six-year-old baseball team like they are getting paid for a living, but I have had about all I can stand of the politically correct, outcome-based thinking that never keeps score and gives the entire league a "participation trophy." Please! By never allowing our children to taste defeat, disappointment or the consequences of poor performance, we are unnaturally prolonging their childhood. In fact, we are creating codependent, self-centered children who think everyone owes them something, and pretty much guaranteeing that they will never get along with their boss, their spouse or their coworkers.

Here are a few ideas on how to create a secure environment that produces dependable adults. You know, the kind that move out of your house before they turn thirty; the kind that stop mooching off you, get a job and stay out of jail.

Build Accountability

We have to start by helping our children understand that they are accountable first to God. The Bible refers to this as "reverent fear for God." This means you must respect and revere God and keep Him at the center of your life. You will not always understand everything about God because He is far too vast for our finite minds to comprehend. You can know Him though. He loves us and demonstrated it in the person of Jesus Christ. Always teach your children to approach Him with reverent fear because we are accountable to Him.

Children should also learn that they are accountable to the human authority in their lives. They will not always agree with said authority, but they need to learn how to respect those with whom they disagree. It is possible to respect others without fearing them; conversely, we can also fear others without respecting them. Our children should learn to fear only God, to respect all people and to cower before no one. We are to stand in awe of God and his creation, while admiring the accomplishments of others, congratulating them for the good things in their lives. Admire and congratulate without worshipping or being intimidated.

We must also teach them that they are to be accountable for their actions. Do not coddle them when they get into trouble. By the same token, don't overreact when they do childish or foolish things, because that is what kids do. By letting children experience the consequence of their actions – bad as well as good – you will instill a spirit of independence in them that will help them become the adults they need to be.

Build Core Values

Children learn core values from how we live rather than from what we say. If I say that I value the Bible but I never read it with my family, never have a visible quiet time, never talk about issues from a biblical perspective and completely ignore what the Bible says, then my family will know that the Bible does not really have a central place in my thinking. No matter how much I complain about the lack of Bible training in the younger generation, my children will know that I really don't live by the Bible's precepts, so they probably won't either.

Do not be shocked if your children disregard your teachings about life if your actions are based simply on culture rather than the constant foundation of the Bible. Culture is constantly changing, like the shifting sand of Jesus' parables. The Bible never does. If your family life is not rooted in the Bible's teachings, it is most likely rooted in culture. That means that the current culture will have a greater influence on how your children behave than will Jesus and his word.

In addition, if my church attendance is based more on convenience than conviction, that means that I am a Christian consumer constantly sucking the church dry without ever serving. If that is true, my behavior is showing my children that worship is not a core value. If all I do is complain about the programs of the church without ever being a part of the solution, I am helping my children learn the core value of selfishness and pettiness rather than servanthood and true worship. That conveys the message that God is an add-on to my life and worship is optional; I partake if it meets my needs.

No wonder so many young people leave the church. They have not been taught the core values of worship and community. They have learned that the church is all about them and their agenda rather than about following Jesus Christ and glorifying God. Unfortunately, they learn these core values from what we do rather than what we say. I could go on with a list of values that we need to teach our children – service, generosity, sexual purity, honoring marriage, loving people, faith – but you get the message. Wise choices grow from good core values. We must model and teach these core values if we want to protect our children from the consequences of unwise and harmful choices.

Set Up Biblical Boundaries

One of the great challenges of parenting is setting up boundaries for our children that are biblically based and consistent. Most of our boundaries and rules should come from a biblical principle. Let me illustrate what I mean with two principles that are taught in the Bible: wisdom and sexual purity. Many verses teach us to live wisely and make wise choices. There are also many verses that command us to have lots of sex with our spouse but refrain from sex with anyone else. Here are several ways that I set up boundaries that are based on biblical principles and commands.

Let's take the principle of sexual purity. My goal for my children is that they live a life that pleases God and that they enjoy God's best in their sex lives. I want them to be disease-free, guilt-free and regret-free. I want them to enjoy a fulfilling and satisfying sex life with their spouse, and hopefully, one day to present me with grandchildren. So how do you set biblical boundaries with that principle in mind?

Since there is no verse about dating ages in the Bible, I have to set boundaries with the principle of sexual purity in mind. Each child is different and each family will have a different set of rules, but the principle is sexual purity and the goal is a fulfilling sex life within marriage. So that principle helps guide me on what age to allow my children to begin dating, what places they are allowed to go, what kind of movies I let them watch and what kind of activities I think are appropriate for them to fulfill the principle of sexual purity. Should I let my daughter go to a graduation party? The Bible doesn't say specifically, but I can let biblical principle guides the boundaries that I set.

Let's look at the principle of living wisely. The Bible doesn't address a lot of issues, like what time curfew should be, how much television your children should watch and how much allowance they should receive. I can base all of my boundaries for my children on the "wisdom" principle. The question is not, "Is this wrong?" but "Is this wise?" It is not necessarily a sin to let your fourteen-year-old have a friend over on a school night and stay up watching movies until 2:00 a.m. I think you would agree, however, that it is not wise. In the long run, that kind of decision consistently made will hurt your child's performance in school. They will do poorly in class, perhaps fail, and struggle to get a good job because they did not get a good education. Is it sinful? No. It is just very unwise and violates the principle of living wisely. A little applied wisdom can save you and your child from a truck load of regret.

Most parents understand that a huge part of our task is to create a safe environment for our children in this unsafe and dangerous world. Ironically, overprotection actually leads to vulnerability. When we overprotect we are unnecessarily exposing our children to even greater dangers. On the other hand, under protecting by failing to hold them accountable for their actions, not instilling core values and failing to set biblical boundaries based on Bible principles exposes our children to a far more sinister danger than the physical type. Our job is to protect them at any cost so that our little arrows can fly unhindered to Christ.

CHAPTER ELEVEN
Respect the Agitator:
Don't Rush the Washing Machine

Parenting is a lifelong process. The roles change as your children get older. You will undoubtedly move from parent to mentor when they become adults, but you will always be their parent. You will always fret and worry over them, but I hope you are mature enough to keep that to yourself when they are grown. That self-control will go far in keeping the relationship open and civil.

Unfortunately, there is no checklist of things to do to guarantee your kid will turn out right. Every person has a sin nature and we all must give account for our own lives. The big idea that we must always come back to is the importance of a relationship with God. What did Moses say? He told us to be careful and remember the Lord. It comes down to that one thing.

You and I can have different approaches but success comes from our relationship with God. If your children are already grown, you must depend on God for help, since your era of direct influence has pretty much passed. If your children are young, you have to start now releasing them to God at the right time. It is a process and is never easy. Letting that arrow go so that it hits the target requires good timing and lots of faith. But depending on God makes the transition easier.

Lessons From the Spin Cycle

Have you ever watched a washing machine? Probably not, because you are normal. But I am not. I do weird things all the time, like stare at cleaning equipment and think about how much it is like life. It's a preacher thing, I guess. Anyway, back to the amazing machine that helps me smell fresh when I am in public. Washing machines have cycles. If the machine skips a cycle, the clothes do not get clean, or they get clean but take forever to dry. The machine has a cycle to fill up with water. It has a cycle that beats the heck out of the clothes to knock the dirt out. Last is the spin cycle. I love that one. Spinning out of control but under control at the same time. In the end, when you go through all the cycles, you get clean clothes.

I think children are a lot like washing machines. I do not mean that they spin around until they're dizzy, make obnoxiously loud noises and do the same things with mindless repetition. I mean that children have to go through all the cycles in order to be a finished product. If you skip a cycle you get grownup kids who aren't completely "finished." Rush the process and your offspring will smell ... well, funky.

Let the cycles do God's work. First, your children will need to fill up sometimes. Those are fun times. They always have to go through the cycle of filling up so that they learn to enjoy God's presence as well as His presents. Make sure that you provide plenty of time for them to appreciate God's goodness and grace. I guess that is the most important part of the process. Then sometimes you will notice that they are getting the crap beat out of them. That is very difficult to endure as a parent but that, too, is necessary for the cleansing process. The agitator is used in this cycle. My wife told me that is what that spinning thing is called, the agitator. If that does not describe the process of growing up, I don't know what does! Sometimes you feel like you are the clothes and your children are the agitators. Don't worry. That cycle doesn't last forever.

I love the spin cycle, when things are going so fast that it feels like they are spinning out of control. Kids feel like this a lot, especially as they get older and take on more responsibility. While we don't want to take the entire margin out of their lives, we do want them to experience enough of life to give them the wisdom to make their own decisions. Like I said before, rescuing them too much will rob them of the chance to learn about how the world works.

"Ritchie, what is your point?" you ask. Just this — don't rush the washing machine. The cycles will end when they end. If you rush the process you get sour smelling kids. If you try to skip a step your kids won't get all the experiences or training they need. I see lots of parents today making this mistake. They either try to skip a step or constantly repeat a step. You can't do it. Let it go.

By the way, parents, we go through cycles for growth, too. Sometimes you just fill up and you never want to leave that cycle. The next thing you know you are getting the sense beat out of you. Sometimes God throws so much stuff at you so fast you feel like you are spinning. Kim and I still talk about the "filling up" we experienced by smelling that new baby smell when we brought our first child home from the hospital. We laugh, because it seems like about a minute later we were freaking out over her graduation. Spinning. Fast. Wrung out. That is what parenting feels like to me sometimes.

Maybe God has chosen to throw things at you kind of fast lately. You are going through spinning cycles and are trying to keep up with the growth. What do you do? You embrace it. God is growing you, He is taking away the crud, and sometimes He tosses you around a bit to get you all the way clean. No matter what cycle He is putting you through right now, you will be fine. God is in control. He knows what He is doing and He has never skipped a cycle or rushed the washing machine. Don't you rush it either.

Chapter TWELVE
Stay on Your Knees

Paul the Apostle writes these words to a group of Christians: "Never stop praying" (1 Thessalonians 5:17, NLT). He is teaching them how to live in the light of Jesus' return. His message is that Jesus is coming again and He is coming soon, so these are some things you need to put really high on your list of priorities. One of those high priorities is that we need to keep on praying.

If that phrase were simply a piece of advice it would be some really, really good advice. We need to pray and keep on praying. We need to keep on praying about everything because our time is short. The truth is, he is not giving out a list of suggestions. This is not like the comment card at the local Sizzler Steakhouse. He is not asking for feedback or for us to add this activity to a list of best practices. He is saying that we had better get to praying and never stop. This is a command for believers. We should pray about everything. That includes praying for our children.

If you could only read one chapter in this book, this is the one I would want you to read. I think it is the most important. More than anything else in this book, we need to learn how to pray for our children. Do not misunderstand what I am saying. I am not saying we need to read books on prayer, or go to seminars on prayer or even to hear more sermons on prayer.

Jesus hated ritualistic, longwinded and meaningless prayers. He said they were not real. He loved the real kinds of prayer – the kind from the heart. He taught His disciples to pray meaningful, to-the-point prayers. He healed lepers when they asked to be healed. He opened blind eyes when people with no theological training simply asked. He saved Peter from drowning when Peter prayed one of the most effective prayers in the Bible: "Lord, save me!" I think God loves it when we get real with Him and get to the point. Not that He does not have the time to listen to fancy language, He just wants us to clear the fog and really talk to Him. He already knows. He just wants us to depend on Him. I think that is the kind of prayer that works best when we pray for our children.

I can think of at least one time in my life when I did not need anyone to teach me how to pray, nor did I depend on my theological training. It just came naturally. I had recently become the pastor of my first church and I was at the church office doing some work. Brittney and Brandon, who were nine and seven at the time, were in the room next to me. Suddenly Brittney came into the room and said in her nonchalant way, "Dad, Brandon is choking." I jumped up and ran to the next room, not knowing what to expect. To my horror I saw my son choking and gasping for air. He could not breathe or talk and he looked like he was about to pass out. Apparently he had been jumping around the room with a bolt in his mouth and had accidentally sucked it into his windpipe.

I grabbed him and held him close as I tried to do the Heimlich maneuver on him. I thought that I could feel the life ebbing out of him. I was desperate. At that moment I did not use fancy words or try to follow a cute pattern for prayer that I had learned in seminary. I did not struggle to find the right thing to say. All I could say was, "Oh, God, please don't let my son die!"

Just as suddenly as it began, it ended. The bolt became unstuck and he began to breathe again. When his airway cleared, we thought he had swallowed the bolt. It actually had gone into his lung. We took him to the doctor, who said everything was fine. About a week later, Brandon got a terribly high fever. We rushed him to the hospital. They x-rayed him and saw the bolt in his lung. The surgeons performed emergency surgery, after which they informed us that he had pneumonia and that if we had waited until the next morning to bring him in he probably would have died.

Stripping the Pretenses

That experience helped me to see prayer in a new way. The pretense was stripped away and I really learned what it meant to pray. Prayer is not about rituals or even about using the right words. Prayer is pouring out your heart to God in the simplest, most basic way. It does not have to be pretty. It can even be primal. Whatever it is, it must be real.

What are the real prayers that you are uttering for your children? Are you praying for them to behave or not to embarrass you? I believe that is the real motivation behind many of our prayers. Often we pray selfishly, not about what is best for them or what will bring glory to God, but about how we can be the most comfortable and the least bothered. I am afraid that we rarely pray real prayers for our children.

I want to encourage you to pray and to keep on praying real prayers for your children. Sending up specific, meaningful requests to God is the most important thing we can do for them. When I do all I can do it is simply *all I can do*. When I pray, I get God involved and then He does what *only He can do*. He can do much more than I can. So keep on praying. Don't ever give up on your children no matter what circumstances look like. When everyone else believes that they are too far gone or hopeless, do not believe it. They may be beyond your reach, but they are never beyond God's reach.

Father, I pray for the person reading this book. I pray that You would encourage them and let them know that good parenting can be easier than they think. Help them to walk in obedience to Your Word. Help them to draw from their relationship to you. Bless the married couples and the single parents who are looking for some hope for their children. I pray that You will reveal Yourself to be faithful and that You will empower them to be great parents. May they have the patience and faith to let Your cycles do their work. Most of all I pray for their children. I pray that they will be like arrows that are released to You. May they hit the target right in the bull's-eye and live lives that are pleasing to You. In Jesus name I ask this prayer, Amen!

About the Author

Ritchie Miller is the founding pastor of Avalon Church in McDonough, Georgia, a suburb of Atlanta. Avalon began on September 9, 2001 with nine couples and has grown to thousands of worshippers. He is also founder and CEO of Avalon HOPE, a non-profit, humanitarian-aid and mission organization. Avalon HOPE gives humanitarian aid to thousands of needy families, plants churches, trains pastors, helps orphans, and supports evangelism in Georgia and around the world. Ritchie is also an avid blogger.

You can learn more by visiting . . .
www.avalonchurch.net or www.ritchiemiller.org.